Foreign Investment and Development in Liberia

PRAEGER SPECIAL STUDIES IN
INTERNATIONAL ECONOMICS AND DEVELOPMENT

Foreign Investment and Development in Liberia

Russell U. McLaughlin

Department of Economics
Drexel Institute of Technology

FREDERICK A. PRAEGER, Publishers
New York · Washington · London

The purpose of the Praeger Special Studies is to make specialized research monographs in international economics and politics available to the academic, business, and government communities. For further information, write to the Special Projects Division, Frederick A. Praeger, Publishers, 111 Fourth Avenue, New York, N. Y. 10003.

FREDERICK A. PRAEGER, *Publishers*
111 Fourth Avenue, New York 3, N.Y., U.S.A.
77-79 Charlotte Street, London W.1, England

Published in the United States of America in 1966
by Frederick A. Praeger, Inc., Publishers

TO

BETTE ANN AND BRUCE

CONTENTS

LIST OF TABLES

PREFACE

This study of the Liberian economy and the role of
foreign investment in its economic development was begun in
1955 and formed the basis of a Ph. D. dissertation, published
in 1958. I had the good fortune to visit Liberia in 1956 in
order to gather otherwise unavailable data and to observe the
operation of public and private investment in progress. In
1963, I returned to Liberia for an extended stay of eighteen
months.

The second visit gave me the opportunity to draw
contrasts between the state of the economy in 1963 and 1955.
Many changes, both large and small, were immediately
apparent, and others revealed themselves after a short while.
New faces worked along with or had replaced those remem-
bered from before. Paved roads had replaced dirt paths.
Traffic lights controlled almost every intersection; and traffic
jams, manifesting a Hirschman disequilibrium between public
and private investment, were a common occurrence. The
road to Ganta was paved for a distance of 100 miles compared
to a distance of only 10 miles beyond Monrovia in 1955. Iron
ore had replaced rubber as the principal form of foreign
investment and income. The United States foreign aid mission was several times larger than in 1955, and the United
Nations economic assistance had also expanded significantly. A sense of urgency and impatience, which was just
beginning to appear in 1955, had, by 1963, permeated the entire
Liberian society.

Despite this, broad sectors of the economy had remained
largely untouched. Life in villages beyond the limited sphere
of influence of roads continued in its unvarying traditional
fashion; the remote villages appeared to have remained unpene-
trated by the sprawling effects of a growing money economy.

The central feature of the Liberian economy is the pre-
dominance of foreign investment in the private sector, and
foreign, particularly United States, aid in the public sector.

This study attempts to define and delineate the role which
foreign public and private investment have played in Liberian
economic development. The study is made against the back-
drop of two personal visits to Liberia at two relatively widely
separated dates. While 1955 does not qualify as the year of
the Rostovian take-off for Liberia, it does provide a convenient line of demarcation between the "old" Liberian
economy and the "new" one. It may be argued that certain
earlier dates had much greater economic significance for

Liberia than this one, but the fact remains that it was not until after the mid-1950's that the concatenation of these forces enabled economic change to become a continuous process instead of the series of sporadic incidents it had been before.

One brief preparatory note on methodology may assist the reader. There are two basic questions which immediately come to mind regarding the relationship between foreign investment and domestic economic development. The first deals with the positive contribution of such capital--and the entrepreneurship which accompanies it--in such diverse ways as employment, training, incomes paid or generated, tax payments, and induced domestic investment, to mention only a few of the many possible positive effects. The second fundamental question centers upon the limitations on the role of foreign investment in the total developmental process of the host country. Both of these basic issues underlie the entire discussion, and form the theme which, it is hoped, will bind together the diverse elements of the entire study.

No author is solely responsible for his product. Those persons, both Liberian and American, who extended personal, professional, or financial assistance to me in 1955-56 have been publicly thanked elsewhere. I trust that they are fully aware of my indebtedness to them, and that they will not be offended by not being specifically cited here.

During my second sojourn to the "Land of the Pepper Bird," I was privileged to discuss the multitude of issues which surround the topic of this study with Liberian officials, private business representatives, and many other people. To all of these, I extend my thanks and appreciation.

I wish to thank Dean James M. Parrish, Dean of the College of Business Administration, Drexel Institute of Technology, Philadelphia, Pennsylvania, who actively supported this research, particularly by discovering funds in his budget with which the typing and supply expenses were financed.

Miss Irene McClean, who typed the final draft, utilized her strategic position to rectify the editorial shortcomings of a former teacher.

To my wife and my children, for both leaving their home to live in Liberia for nineteen months, and for their cooperative, if not joyful acceptance of the lack of a husband and father during the final writing of this volume, I offer a very special "thank you."

Needless to say, in spite of all of the assistance which I have received, the responsibility for errors is entirely mine.

THE LAND

Geography

Location and Terrain

The Republic of Liberia is located on the west coast of
Africa between $4^{\circ}32'$ and $8^{\circ}50'$ north latitude and $7^{\circ}32'$ and
$11^{\circ}32'$ west longitude. Its neighbors are Sierra Leone on
the west, Guinea on the north, and the Ivory Coast on the
south. For the most part, Liberia is rolling country with
few well-defined mountains and valleys. Dr. George W.
Harley describes five geographical belts, their lines of
demarcation running roughly parallel to the coast line. The
first of these belts is the coastal plain which is broken up
by lagoons, marshes, and tidal creeks. Several high prom-
ontories--the most famous being Cape Mount, Cape Mesarado, and Cape Palmas--highlight an otherwise flat and low
coast line. Behind the coastal area is a belt which extends
fifty to eighty miles inland and rises only slightly above sea
level. This is the area in which rubber production is cen-
tralized. A narrow band follows which marks the rise to
the African plateau. Steep hills and escarpments rising
sharply for several hundred feet characterize this zone.
The next zone is a dissected plateau with very low population density, even for Liberia. The final belt consists of
mountains, including the Nimba range.[1] Six large and several small rivers drain Liberia. These are slow moving
due to the relatively slight grade of five to ten feet per mile.

Climate

Liberia has two distinct climatic seasons of about equal
duration. The dry season extends from October to April,
and the rainy season runs from May to October. One
writer has reported that Liberia has the greatest amount of

rainfall of any part of the world with the possible exception
of eastern Nigeria. [2] Average annual rainfall in Monrovia
is about 150 inches. At Harbel, it drops to 126 inches; and
at Ganta, the annual average is 60 inches. [3]

Temperatures are fairly constant, ranging between 75°
and 90° in Monrovia. As one moves inland, he finds the
average temperatures are slightly lower but with a greater
daily range than on the coast. [4] Coupled with these temperatures is a relatively high humidity which averages 86 per
cent to 75 per cent during the wet and dry seasons respectively in Monrovia. The harmattan, which occurs in late
December and early January, lowers the relative humidity
considerably; but the relief is offset by a high concentration
of dust in the air. The effect of the combination of these
weather conditions is a much lower amount of sunlight than
one would expect for a tropical climate. Church reports
that in Freetown the average daily amount of sunlight is only
slightly more than six hours. In addition, the combination
of overcast, mist, and dust serves to filter out ultraviolet
rays from the sun. [5]

The economic effects of this climate are readily apparent
to the observer. The heavy rains leach the soil, wash out
nutrients, and erode the land, leaving gigantic washes and
gullies. Transportation, even on paved roads, is slowed
down. On all but the very best laterite roads transportation
becomes virtually impossible during the wet season. Out-
door construction ceases during this same period, and equipment deteriorates rapidly, especially on the coast where the
rain and humidity are aided and abetted by salt spray. Poor
drainage in many areas provides an ideal breeding ground
for the anopholes mosquito, the host of malaria. Other
disease-bearing insects, including the tsetse fly, also find
this climate exceptionally suited for breeding. Finally, the
general climate causes a general slowing down of the pace of
life by both Africans and Europeans alike. [6]

Soils

The most common characteristic of Liberian soil is the
presence of laterite or latersols. Other soil types are
half-bog, gray hydromorphic, lithosol, alluvial, and coastal
sand. [7]

In addition to the loss of fertility by natural causes, the
"shift farming" or "bush fallowing" method of subsistence
agriculture practiced in Liberia, as in all of tropical
Africa, causes a severe loss of nutrients. A slight offset to
this loss is the gain of minerals from burning of the bush.
However, even after burning, the phosphorous content averages forty to fifty pounds per acre compared to one to three
hundred pounds per acre in the United States. [8]

Natural Resources

About 9 million acres, or more than one third of the total
land area, are covered with high bush--virgin forests which
form a solid canopy over the land. In addition, 5 million
acres are covered with broken stands of trees of merchant-
able size and type. The total number of species in these
forests has not yet been determined; but 235 species have
been identified, of which about one hundred are salable. [9]
Eight National Forest Reserves, aggregating 3.2 million
acres, have been surveyed and reserved for forestry operation on a sustained yield basis. These forests contain 140
billion board feet of marketable lumber, and in full operation could yield 2 billion board feet per year. [10]
At the present time, the most valuable natural resource
of Liberia is her iron ore. The first deposit to be commercially exploited was at Bomi Hills, estimated to contain
300,000,000 tons of ore with a purity exceeding 66 per cent.
The largest deposit discovered to date, however, is in the
Nimba Mountains, close to the Guinea border. The size of
this deposit is not certain, but some guesses run as high as
1 billion tons. The operating company expects to produce
7 million tons per year for at least thirty years. Other
deposits currently under development are in the Bong Mountain and the Mano River areas.
The mining of gold and diamonds is also of economic
significance. Gold production reached a peak in 1943 when
exports of more than 30,000 troy ounces were recorded.
Exports have declined since that date, but how much of this
is due to less production and how much to smuggling (and
hence non-reporting) is not certain.
No other commercial exploitation of mineral deposits has
been undertaken. Traces of manganese, columbite,

tantalite, copper, zinc, chromite, graphite, lead, pyrite,
and corundum have been discovered; but certain knowledge
of whether any of these are present in commercially profitable amounts must await the completion of the geological
survey presently under way.

THE PEOPLE

Population

In the past, estimates of the population of Liberia varied
widely from a high of 2.5 million to below 1 million, a
diversity caused by the lack of a census of any sort prior to
1962. While results of the 1962 Census have not been made
public, reliable estimates place the population at slightly
more than 1 million people.[11] A population tally of 1 million
yields an average density of 23.5 persons per square mile.
This compares with a population density in Sierra Leone of
62, in Guinea of 21, and in Ivory Coast of 20.8. The
Liberian figure is slightly more than half that of Ghana,
about 30 per cent of the Nigerian figure and equal to the density of Kenya.[12] Average densities, however, tell only a
partial story. Concentrations of population are found in
Monrovia with 88,000 inhabitants, Bomi Hills, Harbel,
Gbarnga, and the Kolahun-Voinjama area. Roads appear to
be a major factor in determining population location and the
location of economic activity. Along the main road from
Monrovia to Guinea and northward from Gbarnga to Zorzor,
Voinjama, and Kolahun, densities are reported to be mostly
over 50 and as high as 150 per square mile.[13]

Land-Labor Ratios

The aggregate land-labor ratio in Liberia is considerably
below that in Europe or Asia, and it may seem that Liberia
is unencumbered with a "population problem" such as that
found in China or India. The phenomenon of "disguised
unemployment" which characterizes many underdeveloped
countries is certainly not present in Liberia.[14] Nevertheless, the peculiar method of subsistence farming in Africa

poses a paradox. Under this method of farming, land is
cleared anew annually for a rice crop after which it is
allowed to return to bush for a period of from eight to
twelve years. Therefore, for each acre of land actually
under cultivation at any one time, about ten acres of land
are lying fallow. About 43 per cent of the total land area,
or about 10. 3 million acres, is estimated to be allocated to
tree crop and subsistence agriculture. [15] With at least 8. 5
million acres devoted to subsistence agriculture, and hence
under bush farming rotation, densities of either 65 or 650
per square mile of cultivated land are calculated, depending
on whether one uses the land actually under cultivation at
any one time or the total land area utilized to produce an
annual crop. As indicated later (pp. 22 - 23), the effective
bottleneck to agricultural development in Liberia is the
labor supply and the level of technology, rather than land.
Land is cultivated too extensively by subsistence methods so
that a condition of land underemployment best describes the
rural agricultural sector. The marginal productivity of land
is low, but this is because it is under-utilized rather than
over-employed.

Population Growth

Whether population in Liberia is growing, declining, or
is stationary--and if growing, at what rate--is unknown
because only one census has been taken. While this census
provides the researcher with more demographic data than
heretofore was available, there are no bench marks to permit quantitative comparison and measurement of population
changes. Three important factors which will affect the rate
of population growth in the future may be qualitatively noted,
however.

Health and Sanitation

Improvement of personal health conditions and longer
lives are both ultimate ends as well as means to increased
economic productivity and incomes. An authoritative
source reported to the writer that the average life span in
Liberia is less than forty years. One cause of the low average figure is an extremely high infant mortality rate, which

reaches 70 per cent of children under one year of age in
some areas. [16] In addition, there is a very high death rate
among mothers at child birth. [17] The children who survive
the first year are faced throughout their lives with a multitude of diseases, the effect of which are in turn intensified
by poor diet and sanitation coupled with primitive beliefs and
practices which often times do more harm than good to the
patient. [18] The most common disease is malaria, a killer of
children, and a debilitating agent of adults. [19] Yaws once
was as prevalent as malaria, but this disease has been all
but eliminated by a concerted program of eradication.
Enteric diseases, elephantiasis, hookworm, schistosomiasis,
and tuberculosis are still quite common, however. The
onslaught of viral and bactericidal diseases on the Liberian
is abetted by nutritional deficiences, particularly hyper-
porteinosis, which reduces the individual's resistance to
infection, and deters his recovery. As these health problems are solved, more people will survive infancy and live
longer. As a result, the population will grow, and it will be
a more productive one.

Demonstration Effect

Partially offsetting the positive impact of improved
health and diet conditions on the population is the possibility
that as income expands, a social check on the growth of
population will appear. Ever since Malthus' Essay on
Population, economists and others have debated the causes
and nature of population growth. It is safe to assert that
even in 1965, they have not reached agreement on the
answers to this question. Yet income growth is accompanied at some point by a conscious desire to limit the size
of families. This does not imply that the Malthusian
Spectre will not continue to be a threat to rising per capita
incomes in many parts of the underdeveloped world. The
same pessimistic picture as one sometimes finds elsewhere
does not seem to exist presently in Liberia. However, even
if a rapidly growing population can for some time be absorbed
by that economy, there are bits of evidence which indicate
that at least some Liberians are beginning to regard children
as an economic liability, in spite of whatever other benefits
they bestow upon their parents. The more widespread

the belief becomes that rising per capita income is an inverse function of the size of the family, the more conscious limitation of family size there will be.

Migration

Migration in response to economic conditions is a common practice among African peoples. Villages, and often whole tribes, may move considerable distances from their previous home in search of more fertile land. While such movements are generally confined to the tribal domain, these areas frequently span national boundary lines. Having a tradition of migration in response to economic pressures in the past, it is not surprising to find that Liberia has gained or lost population as economic activities improved or worsened relative to other countries.

Karl Meyer has suggested that a decline in Liberia's population took place between 1920 and 1950.[20] Between 1930 and 1940, both Firestone and the Liberian Government, the two largest employers of wage labor at that time, greatly retrenched their operations. It was not until 1946, however, when the contractors for the construction of the Port of Monrovia could not even find enough unskilled labor, that the severity of the population loss became evident. It was particularly difficult at that time to fill the demand for skilled labor from the Liberian population. Expatriate craftsmen, such as carpenters from Brazil, were imported for work on the Port project.[21] Since 1945, the number of aliens employed in Liberia has risen steadily. In 1955, the number of foreign residents totaled 7,500, compared to 4,000 in 1951. In 1956 there were 9,669 aliens registered with the Bureau of Immigration. In recent years the number of aliens has remained at about 8,000.[22] It is reported that many people who left Liberia in the past are returning, but no data is available to document this claim.

Labor Force

The estimated size of the labor force in Liberia is about 350,000 persons, almost all of whom are males. This total comprises some 90,000 persons currently employed in the money sector and 260,000 able-bodied males in the tribal

economy.[23] An estimate of the labor force made in 1953
puts the figure at about 150,000.[24] While it now appears
that this total was too small, an interesting observation was
made at that time to the effect that no more than 50,000 of
these people could be drawn into the money economy without
inflicting serious damage to food production.[25] When the
large movement of labor into wage employment began in
1958, one very noticeable consequence was a reduction of
local food output. In addition, large employers of unskilled
labor such as Firestone and Goodrich have experienced
chronic difficulty in filling all of their openings. While these
occurrences could be explained by other factors, such as the
effect of higher incomes on the increased importation of food
and the nature of rubber tapping which makes it a less-
favored occupation to other jobs, the withdrawal of labor
from the tribal sector was undoubtedly a major factor in the
decline of food production.

One soon discovers in Liberia that most jobs are filled by
men, including many of those which traditionally in the
United States and in many other countries are generally
reserved for women. Since 1955, there has been a marked
increase in the number of women in clerical, teaching and
nursing positions, but men are still dominant in these fields,
except for nursing. This situation is also true among the
ranks of the semi-skilled and unskilled workers. Firestone
and Goodrich have tried for years to interest women in tapping rubber, but with only a handful of women showing any
interest in this employment.[26] In Monrovia and other urban
centers, women often undertake small trading operations, but
with little success beyond a few dollars of income per month.

One reason for the lack of participation of women in wage
employment is that many jobs which they could do are
presently done by young boys. Another is the traditional
place of women in African society which assigns to them
tasks which are for the most part of a lower order of social
acceptability than those performed by men. The spread of
educational opportunities will gradually eradicate the first
source of competition for jobs, and intensified "westerniza-
tion" of society will break down the second one. As the
economy develops, as new and more jobs are created, and as
an increasing number of boys and men spend longer periods
in school to be trained for more productive jobs than they

now perform, the more widely women will be employed in
agriculture, business, and government.

The Supply of Labor

The shape of the labor supply curve in any society is a
function of a multitude of economic and social forces. While
a complete analysis of these determinants of labor supply in
the Liberian case is not possible here, a suggestive list of
relevant factors may be developed.

Wage - The wage rate, in the form of both the money wage
and various fringe benefits, is the incentive most used by
foreign employers to attract labor. While the wage policies
of foreign employers will be examined in detail in Chapter 4,
a few of the issues may be anticipated. There is considerable evidence that West Africans are more wage conscious
than other African workers because of the presence of a
vigorous money economy for many decades in that part of the
continent. If this assumed casual relationship is valid, the
future growth of the money economy in Liberia will be
expected to enhance this responsiveness to money wages.
   There is no scientific evidence of a backward bending
labor supply curve in the area of the present wage scale
among rural workers. Differing utility functions between
individuals is to be expected, and some workers have been
known to refuse overtime, preferring leisure instead. But
just as many, if not most, workers indicate a preference for
additional income. At Bomi Hills, for example, the average
work week is seventy hours; yet the Liberia Mining Company
has experienced no difficulty in hiring workers.

Non-economic Incentives - Significant differences appear
within the aggregate labor supply function between the
attractiveness to workers of specific jobs and/or employers.
The firms experiencing the greatest ease in filling jobs are
those which, given the wage scale, offer jobs in which
workers will be operating or associated with machinery, or
which hire relatively large numbers of employees.
Machinery operation carries considerable prestige, and the
strongly gregarious Liberian has been known to demand a
higher wage if his job requires that he work alone.[27] In

contrast to the ease of finding workers experienced by the
mining company, agricultural firms have experienced a
chronic shortage of workers. While the chief cause of this
labor shortage in commercial agriculture may be currently
attributed to the considerably lower wage scales of that
industry, the same difficulties in hiring large numbers of
unskilled workers were present in the past when the wage
differential between agricultural and non-agricultural
employment was less than it is presently. Firestone has had
a chronic labor deficit accompanied with a high turnover rate
since the mid-nineteen forties. The African Fruit Company
in 1956 could recruit only 900 men while 3000 were needed.
Urban unemployment was not uncommon in 1955. Potential
workers then, as now, sometimes prefer unemployment to
agricultural activity.

Man-Days of Work - The effective labor force in Liberia is
influenced by a variety of official and ceremonial causes of
absence from work. Compulsory military duty causes
absenteeism four times a year plus required appearances of
the militia at special ceremonies. Holidays, of which there
are ten national and at least four international, are accompanied by a shut-down of offices and stores. Funerals, a
common occurrence, lead to the absence of many people,
and in the case of a deceased high government official, a
complete closing of offices.

Labor productivity is also depressed by a high labor turnover rate. The unskilled rural worker often takes a job for
a specific purpose, such as payment of the Hut Tax or a
particular purchase, and quits it upon the realization of this
objective. Production is lost while new workers are
recruited and instructed in their task.

Education

The story of education in Liberia may be summarized as
an activity which has been going on for a long while, but
which has shown little real progress until very recently. No
one index of the level of educational advancement is able to
give a meaningful measure of the complex state of education.
The prevailing level of literacy serves to point up the results
of past educational efforts, and indicates the extent of the

challenge of the future. For the nation as a whole, the number of people classified as literate is about 20 per cent of the total population. If this figure is reduced to 15 per cent to allow for over-reporting, Liberia compares favorably with its immediate neighbors but still lags seriously behind Ghana and Nigeria. [28] Also, this measure shows a marked improvement over 1955 when the estimated literacy rate was about 10 per cent of the population. The highest incidence of literacy is found in Harper City (42. 9 per cent), followed by Robertsport (39. 0 per cent), Nimba (37. 3 per cent), Monrovia (35. 8 per cent), Bomi Hills (34. 3 per cent), and Kakata (34. 0 per cent). At the other extreme, River Cess Territory has only 2. 9 per cent of its population literate. This rate is surpassed slightly by Harbel (4. 8 per cent), Bahn (5. 0 per cent), and Grand Bassa County (5. 8 per cent). [29]

The incidence of literacy or illiteracy correlates closely with school attendance, as one would expect. In Harper City, almost 76 per cent of the population between five and nineteen years of age are attending school. The comparable figure for Robertsport is 70 per cent, and for Monrovia it is 51 per cent. The correlation between school attendance and literacy is not perfect, however. In some regions, a comparatively high illiteracy rate is associated with a high percentage of the school age population attending school. For example, the present literacy rate in Voinjama is about 15 per cent; yet 53 per cent of the school age children in that town are attending school. In Zwedru, the figures are 20 per cent and 63 per cent, respectively. [30]

The recent improvement in the literacy rate and the rising percentage of children in school do not tell the full story of the status of Liberian education today. Educators in Liberia are greatly concerned about the very high dropout rate which at the end of the third grade may reach 70 per cent of those who started school. While the government is building schools rapidly, the system is severely handicapped by a shortage of trained teachers, supplies, and teaching materials--particularly textbooks. It is fervently hoped by the education authorities that as these factors are remedied, the drop-out rates will decline markedly.

The cost to a country of a poorly educated populace is well known and need not be labored here. There is one cost

to Liberia, which while not unique, is sufficiently large to
deserve special mention. Many jobs requiring high and even
middle level skills are filled by expatriates. In some
instances people filling these posts are paid directly from
the budget. Others are financed indirectly by the government through the payment of high salaries by private concessionaires, which reduces tax payments to the Government;
or they are paid by foreign governments or the United
Nations so that the amount of foreign aid available to Liberia
in other forms is diminished thereby. A direct-hire foreign
technician with an annual salary of $8,000 necessitates an
outlay by his employer of about $20,000 because of the need
to transport him and his family to and from Liberia, to
supply housing, a car, and other emoluments. Today's cost
of a weak educational system in the past is extremely high.

LIBERIAN SOCIETY

Two sets of cultural forces, one internal and one external
have combined to shape the social and cultural character of
the Liberian people. While various, and often antithetical,
forces act upon almost all societies, the special character
and strength of the particular ingredients of Liberian society
emanates from the conditions of the founding and subsequent
history of the country. [32]

In 1822 a small body of emancipated slaves from the United
States, under the sponsorship and leadership of the American
Colonization Society, landed on a small island in the mouth
of the Mesarado River. Despite the signing of treaties with
the chiefs of the indigenous tribes, ceding land to the Society
for a consideration, protracted warfare developed almost
immediately over the specific issue of land ownership. The
African conception of land tenure holds that land cannot be
alienated from the tribe. The Colonists, on the other hand,
were imbued with Western principles of the sanctity of contract and the separability of a piece of land from a specific
person or group. [33] Thus, the Colonists thought that they
had bought the land while the tribes believed that they had
only leased it. This difference in the conception of land ownership was only one of a continuous series of difficulties
which arose between the settler and indigenous groups, the

cause of which may be generalized as a cultural hiatus between the two population elements. The Colonists for the most part, while of African descent, had lived in the United States, assimilating part of the culture of eighteenth and early nineteenth century America, and especially those values of the southern planter. Like their former American masters, this group had emigrated in search of political freedom. The accumulation of wealth in land and buildings and the use of hired labor and even slaves were, for both the American and African settlers, the outward manifestations of the achievement of this freedom. Moreover, a great many of the traits which characterized the complete life of the southern planter were neither known nor understood by the Liberian pioneers. Thrift, industry, literary culture, music and art either were not cultivated or became lost to subsequent generations of Liberians. Therefore, while the settlers and their descendants were genetically Africans, they were culturally foreigners; and skin color was not a sufficient reason to cause acceptance of them by the indigenous tribal peoples.

Thus, two Liberians appeared inside the sovereign and geographic boundaries of the one country. One was that of the self-sufficient African, living his traditional life on the principles of his native institutions and amid social conditions natural to him in his indigenous environment. --- The other was that brought into being by the Western settlers with their high ideals and alien cultural inheritance. Circumstances should have converted them to modify and relate themselves to the great mass of the population with its traditions, habits, customs and values. But a different outlook, natural to these repatriated people, dominated their conduct in this historic relationship, and combined with other things, denied them such coveted flexibility. For not only were the Americans bodily transferred to Africa, but a small circle of their cultural or social milieu was transferred intact with them. A small community of contemporary Americanism or Westernism, as it were, was suddenly set upright in a section of surging Africa. [34]

At first by others and then by themselves, the name of

"Americo-Liberians" was applied to this grafted portion of the Liberian population to distinguish them from the native, uncivilized, or aboriginal peoples. For some time this terminological distinction matched the cultural cleavage which characterized Liberia. In time, however, people from tribal backgrounds entered the westernized sector, some to become high Government officials, but most to receive employment in urban areas and, as a consequence, to assimilate some aspects of Western culture. While there are significant and meaningful differences between Euro-American cultural attributes and African tribal cultural patterns, the old terminology no longer aptly demarcates the population groupings associated with these cultural patterns. Furthermore, the old terminology carries the implication of one cultural system being superior to the other, rather than the more proper interpretation of each being an alternative way of life with its particular strengths and weaknesses. Thus, it is better to designate the people who live chiefly in tribal cultural milieu as "rural Liberians", and those who live in cities and towns and who are subject to a strong Western influence as "urban Liberians". [35]

Rural Liberians

Of the 1 million inhabitants of Liberia, nearly 85 per cent live entirely or primarily within a tribal society with its distinctive customs, language, economic activity, and government. Twenty-eight tribes are divided into five ethnic groups. Twenty-eight dialects are spoken with at least of ten of them necessary for a traveler to be understood anywhere. [36] However, since English is the official language of the country, as well as the language of education, and since missionaries and businessmen are mostly English, there has developed a colorful form of pidgin English which is widely used. [37]

Social Structure and Communal Life

The African living in a tribal environment is not just an individual residing in close proximity to other people. He and his family are part of an organic whole, which is the tribe, and welfare criteria stress the well-being of the tribe rather than the maximization of an individual's utility function. The economic importance of this communal life is manifested in the sharing of labor and of products with others. Much productive activity is a joint endeavor, and is directed toward the achievement of a common end for the group. Traditional lines of demarcation separate activities which are commonly performed and owned from those which are individual or family prerogatives. For example, the production of food is a family undertaking, while the erection of a new hut is a cooperative venture even though it is destined for occupancy by a single family.

Many aspects of communalism are carried with the worker should he leave the village and seek work in an urban center. At the same time, a breakdown of mores and habits takes place because of the lack of the tribal sanctions in the cities. Rogueing is quite common in and about Monrovia, but rarely does it take place in the interior. [38]

Urbanized Liberians

About twenty per cent of the population comprise the group defined above as the people who have by birth or by migration adopted a substantial amount of Western cultural habits and attitudes. This segment of the population is less easy to distinguish with generalities than the tribal or rural Liberians. Included in this category are those who form the "elite", who, as such, direct the course of the country's economic and social development. But also one finds in urban areas many uneducated and unskilled people living a semblance of Western life intermixed with tribal village behavior. These people live in tribal groupings, dress as people in the interior, use tribal language amongst themselves, and often live in dwellings of the same type as found in interior villages. While most of the gainfully employed members of this group are in unskilled positions, their increasing employment as clerks, tailors, drivers, and policemen reflects the changes which are touching the lowest socio-economic members of society and affecting their way of life.

The Elite

The most politically significant component of Liberian

society, and certainly its most controversial one is that
small body of people which forms the elite of the society.
These are the people "who occupy the strategic points of
decision-making in the metropolis and control its
decisions. " [39] This definition may be expanded to include
those living beyond the metropolis but who because of position, wealth or education direct the affairs of the whole
country. Historically, the core of the elite has been the
Americo-Liberians and their descendants in and about Monrovia, although in earlier days other coastal cities vied with
Monrovia for leadership.

About twenty years ago, a change began taking place in
Liberia's elite which is still in process. The "first families"
remain very much in evidence in government service and as
large property owners, but they are being gradually supplemented by a new elite. [40] While many members of this
group are descendants of the "old guard", a growing number
of the new elite group are first generation "arrivals", in the
sense that they are the initial members of their family to
have a higher education. While individual differences
appear between members of his new elite group, there are
certain common characteristics held by the leading members.
First, the members of the new elite are comparatively
young, most of them being under forty when they achieve
prominence. Secondly, they hold positions of relative power,
including positions of cabinet and ambassadorial levels.
Thirdly, they have almost all been educated outside Liberia,
primarily in American or British universities. As products
of an advanced technological society, they measure progress
in modern terms and often become frustrated with the older
politicians and their ways of doing things.

PRODUCING CENTERS

The preceding sections have outlined some of the quantitative and qualitative dimensions of the human and physical
resource base of Liberia. The balance of this chapter will
investigate how these resources have been combined in the
principal production sectors, and how the incomes generated by this production have been distributed. The discussion is descriptive and is designed to set the stage for the

analysis of the blending of foreign capital and domestic resources in the subsequent chapters of this book.

The Liberian economy consists of three principal producing centers--subsistence agriculture, commercial agriculture, and mining. Although government and service industries are important sources of employment and income, they exist as activities ancillary to these three principal producing centers.

The Central Position of Agriculture

Liberia is primarily an agricultural country; and as in other economically underdeveloped countries, the production of food for local consumption and of other agricultural products for export is the central economic activity of the country. Until 1950, agricultural exports accounted for 90 per cent of total exports. By 1955, this ratio had fallen to 77 per cent because of the growing importance of iron ore exports. Nevertheless, rubber and other agricultural products continued to dominate the export total until 1962. By 1963, agriculture claimed only 34 per cent of total exports; however, the physical output of rubber, the principal export crop, remained constant during the period 1955 to 1963, the relative decline in value being the result of falling rubber prices along with the expansion of iron ore output.

Another indication of the position of agriculture in Liberia is found in the estimate that 85 per cent of the population live in rural areas. It is reasonable to assume that no less than 75 per cent of the total labor force, or about 260,000 working age males, are employed in subsistence agriculture.

Distribution of land among various uses further indicates the importance of agriculture in the Liberian economy. Of the 27.5 million acres of land area, about 12 million acres are estimated to be arable land.[41] The remaining area is covered by forests or used for towns or roads, or is wasteland. The arable land area is composed of 2 million acres of swamps and valleys suitable for annual crops; 5 million acres of low foothills adaptable to tree crops or extensive annual crops; and 5 million acres of upper hill slopes suitable only to tree crops.[42] The soil, climatic and topographical qualities of this land are described above.

Subsistence Agriculture

In terms of the total number of farms, the most important type of farming is that carried on under the tribal
system of land ownership, or subsistence farming. The
core of the tribal communalism is the tribal lands, ownership of which rests in the tribe as a corporate body. The
control of the use of land is a semi-religious function,
carried out by the chief or some other functionary, but in
any case, the person in charge of the land is not the owner.
43 While the product of a farm belongs to the farmer, he
uses the land only at the pleasure of the chief. If for any
reason, a village, clan, or even a whole tribe migrate to a
new area, the movement is as a unit.

Village agriculture, for the most part, is subsistence
agriculture in that most of the product is locally consumed.
Cash crop production, while it provides a source of money
income with which to pay taxes or purchase imported goods,
occupies a secondary position in village agriculture. A
characteristic feature of both subsistence and cash crop production in the village economy is the relatively small scale
of the operations. Little or no capital is employed, methods
are primitive and often wasteful, and productivity per worker
is low. These characteristics of peasant agriculture are
both the prime economic cause and effect of Liberia's low
per capita income. As long as productivity in the principal
area of economic activity remains low, it imposes a drag
upon the rest of the economy. At the same time, a slow rate
of development in other economic sectors retards the growth
of income in agriculture.

Several factors account for this interaction effect between
village and non-subsistence, or "modern sector", development. For one, the entire country depends upon government
revenues for the provision of infrastructure investment such
as schools, roads, hospitals and so on. Village agriculture,
because it produces virtually no export surplus, contributes
little to such investment. Rather, the villages depend
directly upon public investment, and hence indirectly upon
the rate of private investment in export crops by others, for
infrastructure capital. As a result the subsistence sector

absorbs resources far in excess of its meagre contribution,
and by so doing, indirectly retards other lines of development. Furthermore, villages are generally small and
located some distance apart. This means that economies of
scale from infrastructure investment are not realized in
contrast to large towns or cities. [44]

Also, low productivity and income among tribal people
limits demand and consequently the rate of investment in
manufacturing, since economies of scale cannot be realized
in most industries because of the limited consumer market.
Consequently, increased consumer purchases of manufactured goods are supplied by importers rather than by new
or expanded domestic production.

The most important aspect of the interrelation between
the rate of growth in the subsistence sector and in the rest
of the economy is found in the nature of the production function in subsistence agriculture, and the movement of
resources in response to a growth in non-subsistence
sectors. Examination of this problem requires a description of subsistence farming methods, following which a
hypothesis of the shape of the production function will be
presented.

Production - Because the products yielded by subsistence
agriculture are largely consumed directly by the producers,
only the most crude kind of estimates may be made of the
volume of such production. The output of rice was estimated
to be about 382 million pounds in 1952. [45] In 1955, imports
amounted to 19 million pounds or about 5 per cent of domestic
production, but by 1963 imports of rice totaled 66 million
pounds. This increase in imports is explained by the combined effects of a rise in per capita income, and increased
population, a reduction of domestic planting of rice caused
by an out-migration of labor from villages to urban centers,
and employment in non-food producing activities.

In addition to rice production, the subsistence economy
includes production of cassava, palm oil, vegetables such as
peanuts, eddoes, corn, sweet potatoes, okra, and sugar
cane. Palm kernels are also sold for cash, but rarely are
they cultivated scientifically. Small rubber plantings are
found almost everywhere, but with yields of only 20 to 30 per
cent of those of large plantations. In some sections of the

country small farmers are growing coffee, but the marketing of these products suffers from a shortage of roads and
processing facilities. In the villages, livestock is produced
on a limited scale only. Cattle is found in numbers only on
the coast in Sinoe and Grand Bassa Counties. Goats and
chickens appear everywhere, but generally they are not
raised for sale by the subsistence farmer. Fishing is a subsistence activity but not well developed in inland rivers.
The introduction of fresh water fish which may be grown in
village ponds has made some, but not significant, headway.

Rice Production Methods

The most widely publicized feature of subsistence rice
production is the technique of rotation known as "bush
fallowing. " A rice crop is initiated with the clearing of a
plot about three acres in size in late January or early February. The men cut all growth with cutlasses and hand axes,
except large or very hard trees. After burning the debris,
women till the ground with simple iron hoes and plant the
seed. Children make a productive contribution by stationing
themselves in the rice field to scare off destructive birds
and animals.

This method of farming, states Kimble....
is, self-evidently, a system with no future that any
ambitious African would feel was worth waiting for.
It is unproductive; its customary crops....are
generally poor in proteins; it leaves hungry mouths;
it provides the cultivator with no incentive to change
his ways; and it is prodigal in its wastage of both
the organic and inorganic resources of the bush. Yet
it was probably the most satisfactory system that
could have been devised by "pre-mechanical" peoples
living in a wet tropical environment. [47]

A further loss to Liberia is in the form of virgin timber
which is cut to "make a farm. " This destruction of forests
results in an annual loss of more than $50 million of mer-
chantable timber. [48]

This method of producing rice utilizes a negligible amount
of capital in the form of a cutlass, an axe, knives and
baskets having a value of perhaps $15 per farm. The

average family farm is about 3 acres in size. The labor
input includes all members of the family in different parts
of the production process which totals about 60 man-days per
100 pounds of rice or about 300 man-days per acre. This
method of rice production is extremely labor intensive with
respect to capital, and also highly labor intensive with
respect to land if the average size farm of 3 acres is considered. The labor-land ratio drops sharply, however, if
the total land area involved in an eight to ten year "slash and
burn" cycle is included. The output from a 3 acre plot is
about 1500 pounds of rice. At the current market price of
$6.50 per 100 pounds, the gross income realized by the
farmer is, at best, only a little more than $100. Measuring
only labor time, the value of labor employed in producing
1500 pounds of rice at 64 cents per day is about $570. Thus,
there is an imputed loss of more than $400 on the typical
rice farm each year. [49]

Production Function for Subsistence Agriculture

The method of rice production described above is one
having a low capital-labor ratio compared to commercial
agriculture and non-agriculture activities. However,
Liberian rice production absorbs a comparatively large
quantity of land compared to Far East rice production
methods. The bottleneck to increased output, therefore,
appears to be labor rather than land as in these other countries. The marginal product of labor in rice production is
low compared to other sectors, but it does not appear to be
zero or close to zero since the necessary capital may be
easily supplied to additional labor. With land as plentiful as
it is, the appearance of additional labor in a village leads to
opening of new farms instead of more intensive applications
of labor to existing farms.

Is the marginal product of labor in subsistence rice cultivation a declining function? From what evidence gathered
from observation and conversation with agricultural specialists would indicate, marginal product of labor is declining,
given the techniques currently in use. If, however, allowance
is made for a change in techniques which are more land and/
or capital using, the answer to this question is not as clear.
An alternate method of production available to many village

rice farmers is the swamp rice technique being investigated and introduced by representatives of the FAO in Liberia. This technique is more land intensive than the bush fallowing method in terms of land actually under cultivation. It uses, for about the same labor input, approximately seven acres of land. The estimated capital input for clearing, diking and preparation is about $100. Experimental yields average 2500 pounds per acre which has a gross market value of about $1140. Since about the same amount of labor is required by this technique for planting, cultivating, and harvesting as for dry rice cultivation, a clear profit accrues to the swamp rice producer. [50]

The FAO technique is, nevertheless, still a small scale and relatively labor intensive technique, utilizing ground so situated that it catches the ground water run-off during the rainy season. In contrast to this method of rice culture is the technique being experimentally introduced at the Gbedin Swamp near Sannequellie. This project is staffed by technicians from the Republic of China and is based on rice production techniques utilized in Taiwan. In comparison to traditional and FAO swamp rice methods, the Gbedin project plan envisages 500 acres of land cultivated by controlled irrigation. The clearing and development cost has been running, so far, at about $500 per acre or more. In addition roads, housing for families, and other facilities are being constructed. The ultimate plan for the project will embrace 3000 acres, with rice being the principal crop but with other foods also being produced. In many ways, this is a major land resettlement scheme and, as such, is difficult to evaluate on economic grounds alone. The yields of rice under experimental conditions with one Chinese technician per five Liberian farmers have been about 7000 pounds per acre. This is achieved by having two crops per year. Capital output ratios have been estimated from a low of 3.4 to as high as 20 depending on the estimated yield under normal operating conditions, and on varying estimates of the total investment cost of the entire project. The project presently is a controversial one, although it is receiving considerable Liberian Government support. As such it is noted here as a third process to be included in the production function. [51]

There are, then, three distinct processes for rice cultivation available to Liberian farmers. The resource ratios differ in all three cases. Subsistence farming and the FAO swamp technique are comparatively labor intensive compared to the Gbedin project, the latter being much more capital-using than the other two. In terms of land actually planted, the subsistence method of agriculture is a less intensive user than are the other rice production methods. However, if allowance is made for the land lying fallow which is a characteristic of this method of production, subsistence or dry rice farming becomes the most intensive land user. So far, however, land supply has not appeared to be a bottleneck to subsistence agriculture production as it is in the Far East. More land suitable to this production method lies idle than that presently employed for the eight to ten year rotation cycle. It is either capital or labor which limit the extension of this process. The capital requirements are so small, however, that it is difficult to imagine a farmer unable to produce the maximum possible output by this method because of a shortage of seeds or implements. It must be concluded, then, that it is the supply of labor which controls aggregate dry-rice output. This assumption, if valid, would explain the reported decline in local rice production which began in 1958 with the migration of labor to diamond mining areas and continued through to the present as alternative employment opportunities in mining and construction appeared after 1959. Also, it sheds light on the reasons for the difficulty reported by Firestone officials of recruiting tappers. According to Firestone officials, chiefs who are reluctant to cooperate in recruiting workers for the plantation allege that if they do so, village food production will decline. Although there may be many hidden reasons for workers not seeking employment on a plantation, one must give some credence to this economic explanation.

Capital shortage also is a superficial reason for the slow development of FAO-type production. However, the funds necessary to finance a major expansion of this type of agriculture are available. The amount spent or planned to be spent on Gbedin would provide the capital for thousands of small swamp rice plots. The lack of knowledge and skill are definite handicaps to the expansion of this production technique.

In summary, it has been noted that subsistence

agriculture output suffers from a labor shortage rather than
from a scarcity of land or capital. This fact helps explain
the low aggregate output of rice and other foods at this level
of production. Furthermore, as labor is drawn into other
employment, the total output of rice may be expected to
decline even further. Village-type farming, therefore, does
not appear to have a marginal product which is zero or close
to zero. Admittedly, productivity is low in comparison to
other rice production techniques, but this is explainable by
the generally poor land which is used, the losses due to rainfall, and other climatic factors as well as the failure to
utilize new techniques because of lack of knowledge, rather
than by a lack of capital in the usual sense of the word.

Commercial Agriculture

Extent

    Commercial farming in Liberia is comparatively wide-
spread as far as the number of farms is concerned, but this
industry is concentrated in both products and ownership. A
commercial farm is defined here to mean one on which the
principal activity is the production of a crop for sale rather
than for use by the farmer. For this purpose, commercial
farms may be divided into Liberian owned and foreign owned.
Statistics are not available to estimate the number, size,
and other dimensions of the Liberian farms, except for a
few large plantations which produce export crops. Firestone
purchased rubber from 2,061 Liberian growers in 1960, but
for some of these producers, rubber is a marginal crop and
the principal activity is subsistence farming. This statistic
also ignores the producers of crops other than rubber which
are marketed either domestically or abroad. Coffee, cocoa,
piassava, poultry, vegetables, sugar cane, and livestock
make up the list of products of the other Liberian commercial
farms.
    The Firestone Plantations Company is the largest of the
foreign-owned plantations, with about 70,000 acres in production. The Goodrich Corporation with 8,600 acres in production in 1962, the Liberian Agricultural Corporation, the
Salala Rubber Corporation, the Liberia Company, and the
African Fruit Company along with Firestone comprise the

list of foreign concessions producing rubber. Table 1
presents some of the relevant comparative data for these
six concessions.

Table 1 : Acreage in Production, Output, Employment,
and Acreage Developed--Liberian Rubber
Concessions

Concession	Acreage in Production (1962)	Output (1960)	Employ- ment (1961)	Acreage Developed
Firestone	70, 000	81, 000	21, 000	102, 000
Goodrich	8, 600	- - -	740	58, 000
Liberian Agric. Corporation	5, 000	- - -	1, 000	53, 000
Salala Rubber	500	- - -	960	15, 000
Liberia Co.	5, 000*	- - -	1, 100	25, 000
African Fruit Company	4, 000	- - -	1, 000	5, 000

*3, 000 acres in rubber, the balance in cocoa (600) and
coffee (14, 000). Production in 1960--41, 000 pounds of cocoa
and 115, 000 pounds of coffee.

Source: Office of National Planning, Republic of Liberia,
Annual Report, 1960-1961, p. 25a.

Capital Investment

The only agricultural enterprise for which an estimate of
capital investment has been made is Firestone. The
recorded figure is $32 million dollars, which includes proc-
essing facilities, roads, housing, schools, hospital and clinics,

and other installations. Since much of this investment was
made years ago at a lower price level, a doubling of the
figure to the level of $64 million seems reasonable. Based
on 1963 output of 77 million pounds valued at $20 million,
the capital-output ratio appears to be slightly in excess of
three. The Liberian plantations have a much smaller
investment per acre because they utilize Firestone facilities.
For the very large farms with high productivity, the capital-
output ratio would be less than for Firestone; but for most of
the farms, it will be higher because of low productivity per
acre.

Productivity

Since rubber is the most important cash crop for Liberia,
it is the industry which has received the most study and for
which data is most readily available. Firestone stands as
the standard against which the operations of other producers
are measured in all respects. Productivity is usually presented in terms of pounds of rubber per acre of producing
trees, and for Firestone, the daily output per acre is
reported to be slightly more than sixteen pounds. A few
Liberian farms match, and possibly exceed, this figure.
These are large plantations, having economies of scale,
responsible management, and modern technology. As a
result, for these farms, not only is output measured by
weight at a high figure, but the value of their product is
large as well because it is sold in the form of latex which
brings the highest price. Against these few highly productive and profitable farms stands the bulk of Liberian producers having an average output per acre of only five pounds
of rubber. At the present minimum wage for agricultural
workers of 64 cents per day, these farmers are not able to
cover much more than their variable costs and some do not
even accomplish this.

The concentration of Liberian owned rubber production
in indicated in Table 2.   The 79. 3 per cent of these producers with annual sales of less than $1000 receive a gross
income averaging $274.   In contrast, eleven farms, on the
average, gross $110, 000 annually and in the aggregate
account for 21. 9 per cent of gross Liberian income from
rubber farming.

Table 2:   Distribution of Independent Rubber Farms by
           Gross Sales, 1960 (Thousands of Dollars)

Money value of Output	Number of Producers	Gross Sales Revenue	Cumulative % of Total Farms	Cumulative % of Revenue
Under 1	1822	498	79. 3	11. 2
1 - 1.9	181	752	87. 2	17. 2
2 - 4.9	160	503	94. 2	29. 1
5 - 9.9	69	484	97. 2	40. 7
10 - 19.9	31	442	98. 5	51. 2
20 - 49.9	26	762	99. 6	69. 3
50 - 99.9	6	368	99. 9	78. 1
100 and over	5	853	100. 0	100. 0
Total	2300	4662		

Source: Office of National Planning, Republic of Liberia,
Annual Report, 1960-1961, p. 26.

Incomes Generated

The rubber concessions currently are paying about $4. 5 million in income taxes to the Liberian Government, virtually all of which is presently paid by Firestone alone. This figure is subject to annual changes reflecting world rubber prices, and the growth of output as new concessions come into production. Since world rubber prices are exhibiting a secular decline and Liberian output is due to rise, as Goodrich and other concessions come into production, the effects of these two movements will tend to offset each other.

Wages paid by the concessions are difficult to measure because of the inclusion in the total of "fringe benefits". Firestone reports that the average tapper wage plus benefits costs $1. 20 per day. For 21, 000 workers, almost all tappers, this total would yield an aggregate money plus income-in-kind payment of between $9 and $10 million

annually. Other producers, assuming the same wage cost
per worker add $2 to $2.5 million to this total. The Firestone estimate of the money wage component of this cost is
in the magnitude of two-thirds of the total labor cost. Thus
about $8 million in money wages are currently being
injected into the economy of these concessions.

A survey of Liberian rubber farms revealed that the
monthly wage bill of 1714 farms in 1960 was $119,200 or
$1.4 million annually. The estimated profit of these firms
in 1960 was only $200,000 in the aggregate or only about $100
per farm. While the accounting procedures used are subject
to question, this figure supports the claim made previously
that most Liberian rubber farms currently are being operated at a loss.[52]

Mining Industry

Mining is the newest and most dramatic industry to
appear in Liberia. The history of the oldest company,
Liberia Mining Company (LMC), is described elsewhere and
need not be repeated here. This company has reached what
is probably the maximum level of its operation at Bomi Hills
and as such offers the best insight into the resource use of
iron ore production. Liberian-American Minerals Company
(LAMCO) has finally passed through its gestation period and
is currently an operating mine. While between these two
mines there exist some sharp contrasts in input-output
relationships, they, along with National Iron Ore Company
(NIOC) and Deutsch-Liberian Mining Company (DELIMCO)
stand as a third source of employment, production, and
income along with subsistent and commercial agriculture.

Resource Use in Mining

A summary of capital and labor resource employment in
iron ore is given in Table 3. The amount of land area utilized by mining is a much smaller drain on this resource
compared to that by commercial agriculture and forestry.[53]
Investment far surpasses the probable amount in commercial agriculture, but employment is markedly less. These
are generalizations which are intuitively expected given the
present state of technologies in the commercial agriculture

and mining sectors. The average capital-output ratio in
mining is not significantly below that of Firestone, but this
ratio differs substantially between LAMCO and DELIMCO on
the one hand and LMC and NIOC on the other. Several
reasons may account for this variation, such as the distance
of the mine from the coast and changes in both local and
foreign price levels which determine investment cost. However, a major cause of the difference is explained by the
realization by LMC and NIOC of external economies emanating from the Port of Monrovia. While LMC had to build
a railway, the construction cost in 1948-1950 was considerably less than for DELIMCO in 1963. NIOC had only to
extend the LMC railway a few miles to its own site. All
three companies, however, are able to use the Free Port of
Monrovia with additional investment only in special piers,
storage, and handling facilities being required. Had LMC
and NIOC built the entire port at its original cost of $19 mil-
lion, the combined capital-output ratio for the two companies
would be approximately 1. 7 against a combined ratio of 1. 3 ,
as indicated in Table 3. Nevertheless, this revised figure is
still considerably below that of both LAMCO and DELIMCO.
LAMCO's mining site is located more than 200 miles inland,
and the company had to construct a railroad from the mine
to the coast. In addition, a port was built at the western
terminus of the railroad which is capable of handling general
cargo as well as iron ore. The mine itself is located on the
crest of a mountain range, and the ore must be crushed at
this point for transport to the storage bins in Seca Valley by
conveyor belt. All of these factors combined with the higher
level of construction costs in 1960-1963, compared to ten
years earlier, explain much of the difference in the capital-
output ratio between LAMCO and LMC or NIOC.
        DELIMCO has access to the Port of Monrovia. The higher
capital-output ratio for this company is partially explained
by the lower quality ore in its concession. More elaborate
equipment is required by this firm than by the others in
order to pelletize the ore before export.
        The gross output per worker averages $21, 900 and ranges
from $17, 300 at LMC to about $24, 000 at NIOC.[54] These
figures are in sharp contrast to the output per worker ratio
at Firestone which is in the neighborhood of $1, 750. These
differences are reflected in wage rates which in mining

averages between 25 and 35 cents per hour for semi-skilled
workers, in contrast to a base wage of 10 cents per hour at
Firestone.[55]

Table 3: Liberian Iron Ore Investment and Estimated
Production and Employment Capacity

Company	Investment Millions of Dollars	Estimated Capacity of Production		Capital Output Ratio	Employ-ment
		Quantity Millions	Value* of Tons		
LMC	37	3. 0	24. 0	1. 5	1400
LAMCO	220	7. 0	56. 0	3. 9	4000
DELIMCO	100	4. 5	28. 0	3. 6	4000
NIOC	26	3. 0	24. 0	1. 1	1000
Totals	383	17. 5	140. 0	2. 7**	6400

*   Value calculated at $8 per ton.
** Weighted arithmetic mean.

Source: Office of National Planning, Republic of Liberia,
Annual Report, 1961-1962, p. 32 and Annual Report 1962-
1963, pp. 38-39.

Incomes Generated

By 1962, iron ore royalties surpassed income taxes to
become the largest source of government revenue. Production, which had been below 3 million tons per year until
1961, jumped to 3. 7 million tons in 1962, and 6. 4 million tons
in 1963. Estimated production for 1964 is in the magnitude
of 8 million tons. As a consequence, royalties paid to the
Government of Liberia increased, but not as rapidly as output because of a decline in the world iron ore prices, a

trend which is expected to continue for some time. Payments in 1963 totaled $6.8 million in contrast to $5.8 million in 1962. The future behavior of iron ore royalty payments along with taxes paid by other concessions and Liberian producers of export products will hold the key to success of Liberia's economic development effort. This dependence upon a narrow tax base involves dangers which have been revealed by the budget crisis of 1963. This crisis came about when expected iron ore royalties did not materialize partly because of a fall in prices and partly because of a delay in the construction of the LAMCO mining enterprise.

Iron ore mines account for considerably less employment than rubber plantations, but the average wage payment is much higher. LMC employs 1400 workers at a wage of 25 to 35 cents per hour for semi-skilled and from 50 and hour upwards for skilled workers. LMC then pays more than $1.7 million in wages annually. With 6400 Liberians employed by all four mines, the wage bill approaches $7.5 to $8.0 million annually.

TOTAL NATIONAL PRODUCT

A set of income and product accounts has been developed for Liberia for the year 1960. While unfortunately there are no prior or subsequent data of comparable coverage to permit an historical analysis, the present structure of the total economy is suggested by these accounts.

Total wages, salaries, and supplements in that year approximated $47 million. Of this, about $5 million was paid to migrant members of the tribal economy, which supplemented their imputed income of $7.3 million. In comparison, the roughly 82,000 members of the labor force in that year earned $29.0 million.[57]

It is apparent that the distribution of labor income is quite unequal between the tribal and the money sectors of the economy. Profits loom large in the total income picture. Concession profits subject to tax were $39.6 million, in addition to which must be added depreciation and other reserves of $21.4 million. When non-concession profits are included along with the profit of government enterprises, the total profit plus reserves earned by business amounted to

50. 3 per cent of Gross Domestic Product.

Rents also bulk large in the total, and primarily reflect the payments for housing and commercial properties. This is especially true in Monrovia. Property rental is an extremely lucrative enterprise today, and a considerable amount of domestic capital flows into this kind of construction.

Table 4:   Domestic Income and Expenditures: 1960
(Millions of U. S. Dollars)

INCOME	
1. Wages, salaries and supplements	
a. African	33. 7
b. Non-African	13. 2
2. Net money income of tribal households	7. 3
(exclusive of money wages)	
3. Gross business surplus	
a. Concession profits subject to tax	39. 6
b. Other concession surplus (before tax transfers and depreciation, development and contingency allowances, etc.)	21. 4
c. Profits and other surplus of non-concession business firms (Liberian and foreign)	26. 5
d. Profits from government enterprises	0. 8
4. Gross rents	10. 5
5. Net interest (including interest on productive government debt)	4. 2
6. Indirect taxes and fees	15. 7
GROSS DOMESTIC MONEY INCOME AT MARKET PRICES	172. 9

Source: Office of National Planning, Republic of Liberia, Annual Report, 1960-1961, p. 16a.

Table 4 continued: Domestic Income and Expenditures:
1960 (Millions of U. S. Dollars)

EXPENDITURE		
7. Current goods and services		
a. Households in money economy		79. 2
b. Tribal households		12. 0
c. Government		16. 9
8. Gross domestic fixed capital formation		
a. Concessions		31. 0
b. Other business concerns and households		18. 2
c. Government		4. 8
9. Net increase in inventories		10. 0
10. Net foreign investment		0. 8
a. Exports (f. a. s. values)	84. 6	
b. Imports (f. a. s. values)	83. 8	
GROSS DOMESTIC MONEY EXPENDITURE		172. 9

THE USE OF INCOME

Households

The principal source of personal income in Liberia is
wages and salaries, including supplements. Concession
employers are the largest source of this income, paying $20
million per year to Liberians. Government is the next
largest source of labor income. In 1960, wages and salaries
were 32. 6 per cent of the operating budget and 22 per cent of
the total budget. With a total budget of $40 million in 1964
the Government's contribution to total wage and salary income
approximated $8. 8 million. Other private employment
yielded about $9 million in wages.

In addition to wage and salary income, rents and business
income must be added. In 1960 these totaled $10. 5 million
and $26. 5 million respectively. Non-African household

incomes for 1960 were estimated at $13.2 million. All of
these were higher in 1964 than in 1960 by at least 15 per cent.
Thus, for 1964, household income from all sources approximated $95.5 million, composed of the following elements:

Wages and salaries of concessions	20.0
Wages and salaries of Government of Liberia	9.0
Other wages and salaries	9.0
Rents	12.0
Business Incomes	30.5
Non-African Household Income	15.0
(Millions of Dollars)	95.5

At this point, analysis based on empirical evidence
becomes difficult. A high percentage of personal income
after taxes is spent on current consumption. If we assume
that 25 per cent of non-African income and 10 per cent of
Liberia household income is saved (repatriated in the case
of non-Liberians), the average propensity to consume would
be 87.5 per cent. Of this amount about 75 per cent or $62.5
million is spent for imported consumer goods. [58]
The estimated $8 million of Liberian savings must be
further reduced by personal tax payments. This amount
does not exceed $1.5 million per year, however, and leaves a
total of $6.5 million. This figure may be greatly overstated
in the light of the 1960 finding of personal saving in the magnitude of $1.5 to $2.0 million. There is no way of vali-
dating either figure, but even taking the higher one as
presently the more accurate, it represents no more than 3
per cent of the Gross Domestic Product (assumed to be $180
million in 1960). It is reported also that considerable savings
of high income families are exported--a fact which would
reduce the amount available for investment. Real estate
dealing and construction are large claimants on the balance.
Hence, it is apparent that little investment will be financed
by domestic private saving in the foreseeable future. At the
same time, a high propensity to import consumer goods
causes income to be channeled into the hands of those who
are most likely to export personal savings rather than invest
them in Liberia.

Government Spending

Liberia's budget reflects a strong desire to invest in developmental projects of both a capital and service nature, coupled with a conflicting desire to live well and present a desirable "image" of affluence to the world. A study of the present composition of the budget in comparison with past years indicates that a healthy percentage of additional revenues has gone into "developmental activities" in contrast to non-productive expenditures.

Until 1945, income was too small to permit more than debt repayment and the performance of rudimentary operations. Between 1943 and 1947 combined expenditures on education, health, agriculture, public works and public enterprises averaged 23 per cent of total expenditures. From 1948 to 1953, these expenditures claimed between 40 and 50 per cent of the total budget. Since that time the proportion of total outlays so allocated has remained at about the 50 per cent mark. Education has averaged between 10 and 12 per cent of the total budget as has public health expenditures. These totals do not indicate the extent of resources devoted to these functions, however, because of the large share of U. S. and U. N. aid which is devoted to these areas, particularly to education.

The Liberian Government has also been a major investor in tangible capital assets utilizing foreign loans and grants to supplement its own resources. In 1964, capital projects totaling $91 million were in various stages of planning or execution, of which $15 million had been disbursed from either loan proceeds or revenues. $56. 8 million was assured from foreign sources, and $1. 233 million was provided for in the current budget. The largest item in this capital budget was the Mount Coffee Hydro project which will cost $27 million upon completion. The Monrovia Sewer Project, estimated to cost $8 million is the next largest project currently in progress. Three highway projects costing $11. 5 million, the para-medical training center priced at $5. 9 million, and assorted educational facilities costing $7. 1 million are the other principal capital projects currently in process or under serious consideration. [59]

This proposed package of capital construction projects to be financed by either forced saving or by self-liquidating

foreign loans represents a high rate of capital formation for
Liberia. The major danger of this program is that the
repayments of loans plus the increased operating costs
induced by the investments will place an inordinate pressure
on the budget over the next several years. Most of these
projects have a long pay-off period either in the form of
higher incomes or as increased tax revenues. There is little
doubt that in the long run all of these and other subsequent
projects of a similar nature will yield a high rate of return.
But the country is faced with a short run period of austerity
until this happens.

Business Profits

Most business profits earned in Liberia are the property
of foreign nationals. Taxation and royalties tap these
expatriate incomes, but a considerable share is nevertheless repatriated. In 1960, concessions earned gross profits
of $60 million of which more than $20 million was allocated
to various reserve accounts. Of the $40 million of the tax-
able profits which remained, $13.5 million was paid to the
Liberian Government as taxes or royalties. Competent
authority has asserted that tax evasion by other businesses
is widespread, and that by tightening the administration of
the tax laws, a further substantial increase in revenues
could be realized. Tax administration reform is currently
under way, and the unofficially reported high pay-off of this
effort lends substance to these assertions.

FOOTNOTES

1. Mount Nimba is reported by Reed to rise to 4,200 feet.
W. E. Reed, Reconnaissance Soil Survey of Liberia
(Washington: United States Government Printing Office,
June 1951), p. 1. Dr. Harley gives the height as 6,500 feet.
G. W. Harley, Geographical Review, "Roads and Trails in
Liberia," (1939), pp. 447-460.

2. C. R. Orton, Agriculture of Liberia (Washington: United
States Government Printing Office, 1954), p. 3.

3. Orton, op. cit., p. 4, and Reed, op. cit., pp. 3-5.

4. United States Department of Commerce, Basic Data on the Liberian Economy (Washington: United States Government Printing Office, 1955), p. 1.

5. R. J. J. Church, West Africa (2nd ed., London: Longmans, Green and Co. Ltd., 1960), pp. 35-36.

6. See E. P. Hanson, "Problems of Liberia's Economic Development." Speech delivered in Monrovia, Liberia, January 14, 1945.

7. Reed, op. cit., p. 35.

8. Ibid., p. 35.

9. K. R. Mayer, Forest Resources of Liberia (Washington: United States Government Printing Office, 1951), pp. 38-39.

10. H. B. Cole, Liberian Year Book, 1962, Monrovia: p. 181.

11. The figure of 1,000,000 is used by planning officials and will be the total employed in this study.

12. See Church, op. cit., pp. 302, 279, 344. Also G. H. T. Kimble, Tropical Africa (New York: The Twentieth Century Fund, 1962), I, p. 89.

13. Church, op. cit., p. 332.

14. For example, Buck estimates the population density in "Agricultural China" at 340 persons per square mile. J. L. Buck, Land Utilization in China (Chicago: University of Chicago Press, 1937), pp. 5-6. Buchanan and Ellis offer an interesting analysis of the meanings of the terms "over-population" and "under-population" in Approaches to Economic Development (New York: The Twentiety Century Fund, 1955), pp. 256-258.

15. Reed, op. cit., pp. 32-33.

16. Dr. George W. Harley, doctor, anthropologist, missionary and veteran of thirty years of service in Liberia's hinterland, conveyed this information to the writer in a personal interview in 1956.

17. A United Nation's official in Liberia stated privately that at a clinic in the interior with modern knowledge and techniques, six children or mothers die in every ten births. Poor general health and improper prenatal care are ascribed as the chief reasons for this loss.

18. See J. C. Furnas, "The House That Saves Lives," Saturday Evening Post. Reprint by special permission of publisher, 1953.

19. Private conversation with Dr. John Moorehead, Public Health Advisor, USOM, Liberia. The debilitating effects of malaria become apparent almost at once to the visitor in Liberia. He notices many people sleeping most of the day and otherwise not producing; contact with government offices makes him aware of a high absentee rate. The first reaction is to regard this as laziness and irresponsibility. Later he learns that a good share of this sleeping and absenteeism is due to malaria, as well as to general poor health. This initial misinterpretation is partly due to the fact that neither malnutrition nor malaria is openly apparent. The African may have a poor diet, but he does not starve even in the city, since tribal "brothers" are obligated to feed him if they have anything at all. Hence, a kind of "sharing the poverty" occurs. He does not often beg, for the same communal property reason. While one knows that many people are hungry, he will rarely ask for money or food. When this happens, it can be assumed that the situation is extremely bad.

20. Mayer, op. cit., p. 16.

21. E. P. Hanson, Comments on the Five Year Plan for the Over-all Development of the Republic of Liberia, (Mimeographed 1946), p. 7.

22. Conversation with the Director of Bureau of Immigration

in Monrovia in 1956 and Cole, op. cit. , p. 205.

23.   Based on estimates from Office of National Planning,
Republic of Liberia, Annual Report 1963-1964 (Monrovia:
1964), p. 11.

24.   Mayer, op. cit. , p. 16.

25.   For Tropical Africa as a whole, a withdrawal of 1/6
of the labor force would seriously upset the pattern of
traditional agriculture. See Kimble, op. cit. , II, 572-573.

26.   Firestone and Goodrich spokesmen both agree that
women make excellent tappers, generally being superior to
men in their ability to carefully tap a rubber tree.

27.   The writer heard of many such instances. One employer
stated that if he wanted windows washed, he must assign two
boys to the job in order to have it done. The digging of a
well requires four men, two working and two watching and
talking. This situation is reported to be common and is one
form of labor waste in the Liberian economy. It is also
possible that this practice is caused by the need for a large
complement of men to perform strenuous work because of
the low stamina level due to poor health and diet. Or it may
be merely an accepted assumption about Liberian labor,
which is untested.

28.   Liberia had until recently the unenviable reputation of
being the most illiterate country in all of Africa. In 1900,
only three per cent of the population had received any
formal education, and only this number could be presumed
to be literate. Kimble, op. cit. , II, 125.
Literacy Rates for Some Other West African Countries are:

	Per Cent of Population Literate
Sierra Leone	12
Guinea	10
Ivory Coast	16
Ghana	25
Nigeria	25

F. G. Burke, Africa's Quest For Order, (New York:

Prentice-Hall, Inc., 1964), pp. 172-175.

29. Unofficial 1962 Census figures of Republic of Liberia.

30. These figures are undoubtedly overstated, for many
children are known to be registered but not attending school.
Furthermore, children are reported as being in school, but
not registered nor attending. The case of children being in
school but not registered or reported to the census taker as
not being in school but actually attending, is rarely encountered. The education budget which was $2000 in 1920 and
$154,000 in 1946, has risen to nearly $4,000,000 (including
the University of Liberia) in 1964. This expenditure is
augmented by a sizable outlay on education by missionaries,
concessionaires and technical assistance from other
countries and the U. N.

31. See G. W. Brown, The Economic History of Liberia
(Washington: The Associated Publishers Inc., 1941) for a
scholarly analysis of the economic problems of Liberia
before 1940, with particular reference to the relation between
the cultural cleavage of the people of Liberia and the
economic development of the country.

32. The early history of Liberia is described in several
studies. See Brown, op. cit.; Sir H. Johnston, Liberia
(London: Hutchinson and Company, 1906), and C. H.
Huberich, The Political and Legislative History of Liberia
(New York: Central Book Company, 1947). The records of
the American Colonization Society are available in a document entitled African Repository, a monthly publication of
the American Colonization Society.

33. See M. J. Herskovits, The Human Factor in Changing
Africa (New York: Alfred A. Knopf, 1962), Chap. 6
especially pp. 144-146.

34. Brown, op. cit., p. 20.

35. There are, of course, some notable exceptions to this
simple classification. In and around Monrovia, there are
settlements of people living and thinking much like those in

remote interior villages. On the other hand, some wealthy Liberians exemplify the life of the well-to-do American "exurbanite". However, the two main streams of culture are centered in the interior rural villages and the metropolitan areas, respectively.

36. These ethnic groupings are Kru, Kpelle, Mandingo, Kissi and Gola.

37. The Vai language is written in a peculiar script which is Arabic in appearance. A delightful story of the origin of this script is told in Republic of Liberia, Department of the Interior, Legends of the Vai Tribe, (Monrovia: 1954), p. 7.

38. "The most remarkable characteristic of the people in the interior of Liberia is their complete honesty. In all the writer's travels, he never had a single item stolen." T. Holsoe, Forestry Progress and Timbering Opportunities in the Republic of Liberia, p. 21 (Washington: United States Government Printing Office, 1955). Mr. Holsoe states that a cash box was carried, containing coins for dashing chiefs in villages, and for paying wages. The box was headloaded in the morning and not seen again until night, and nothing was missing. Mr. Fahnbullah of the Interior Department stated in a private conversation that people along main roads are now putting doors and locks on their huts, items never found in the deep interior.

39. R. K. Lamb, "Political Elites," The Progress of Underdeveloped Areas, (Chicago: University of Chicago Press, 1952), p. 32.

40. See J. C. Liebenow, "Liberia," in G. M. Carter, African One-Party States (Ithaca: Cornell University Press, 1962).

41. Meier, Oscar, Liberia Annual Economic Report and Summary of Current Economic Information (Monrovia: Legation Dispatch No. 156, September 23, 1948), p. 27.

42. Meier, op. cit., p. 13.

43. D. E. Apter, The Gold Coast in Transition (Princeton: Princeton University Press, 1955), p. 53. Apter's discussion is of the Ashanti in Ghana. While differences in detail occur even between parts of one tribe, the principles of economic organization in all West Africa tribal groups are the same.

44. For example, only eight cities or towns and four territories have a sufficiently large population in the 14 to 19 year age group to warrant construction and staffing of one or more modern high schools without having to provide dormitory facilities, assuming most of the people in this age group attend high school, which they presently do not.

45. United States Department of Commerce, Statistical Abstract, 1952 (Washington: United States Government Printing Office, 1952), p. 927. This production estimate seems reliable, since about 700,000 acres are estimated each year to be planted in rice, and the yield per acre is about five hundred pounds.

46. The rice bird is a major problem to farmers. This bird appears at seeding time and again when the grain is ready for harvest. The writer was told that in French West Africa the birds become such a problem that the Government was obliged to take a hand in controlling these pests, even resorting to dynamiting the bush adjoining rice farms. Despite the most conscientious watching, however, the loss of rice due to rice birds is estimated to be about 20 per cent of a crop. Holsoe, op. cit., p. 10.

47. Kimble, op. cit., I, 133. For a technical discussion of Liberian dry rice farming, see the following sources:

   Orton, op. cit.
   Mayer, op. cit.
   Holsoe, op. cit.
   United States Foreign Operations Administration, Liberian Swamp Rice Production A Success (Washington: United States Government Printing Office, 1955)
   Brown, op. cit.
   Republic of Liberia, Department of the Interior, op. cit.

48. "Since normally the high forest areas which are cleared
for farming will have timber stands of at least 15, 000 board
feet per acre, it means that each year about three-quarters
of a billion board feet are cut down, burned and wasted.
Based on present day regulations, this amount of timber if
processed would give a revenue to the Government of Liberia
amounting to more than $2 million, and if it were sold it
would have a market value of about $50 million. The yield
that the farmers obtain from growing rice on those areas
amounts to about five hundred pounds per acre, with an average price of about $6 per hundred pounds. In other words,
the farmer gets an income of about $30 per acre for his
efforts or only a few cents per hour for his and his family's
working time, compared to $45 per acre which would be the
excise tax obtained by the Liberian Government from the
sale of this timber. If this timber were cut and sold, it
would represent a value of $900. " Holsoe, op. cit. , p. 10.
The government revenue referred to above is from a stump-
age fee or excise tax of $3 per thousand board feet for timber,
planks, and timbers or other partially manufactured wood
products, or $5 per thousand board feet on logs to be exported.
Republic of Liberia, Forest and Wildlife Rules and Regulations , 1954, Reg. 34. Reprinted in Holsoe, op. cit. ,
Appendix II.

49. The foregoing estimates of labor time were made by
agricultural specialists of the United States Operations
Mission in 1955.

50. Data based on personal conversation by the author with
FAO specialists in Monrovia. Similar swamp rice production
techniques are used in other West African countries with a
reported average yield of 820 pounds per acre. If this figure
is used, the Liberian farmer would have a gross income of
$400 and a net loss of about $170 per year. See Church, op.
cit. , p. 100.

51. This information is based upon data found in various
official publications of the Department of Agriculture, Republic
of Liberia, and upon personal conversation with FAO agricultural technicians.

52.   Republic of Liberia, Bureau of Economic Research and
Statistics, Annual Report, 1960-1961, (Monrovia: 1961),
Appendix A.

53.   Ibid. , Tables 1-5, 1-6, 1-7,

54.   These figures slightly overstate the output per worker
since port personnel are not included.

55.   Office of National Planning, op. cit. , p. 12.   Almost
all mining labor is classified as semi-skilled while in
rubber the bulk of the labor force are tappers,   classed as
unskilled labor.   Firestone pays the same higher wage to
semi-skilled labor but this is only a small per cent of their
total labor force.

56.   Republic of Liberia, Office of National Planning, Annual
Report,   1962-1963, (Monrovia: 1963), p. 42.

57. $33. 7 million less $4. 7 million, the second figure
being imputed from the difference between tribal household
expenditures of $12 million and net money income of $7. 2
million.

58.   Based on a preliminary Household Budget Study in
Monrovia.

59.   Office of National Planning, Annual Report 1963-1964,
(Monrovia: 1964), pp. 27-64.

CHAPTER 2 THE OPEN DOOR

For the first 104 years of her history--1822 to 1926--
Liberia received only a slight amount of foreign private
investment and almost no direct economic aid from foreign
governments. Such external investment as there was consisted of loans floated in Europe by the Government at fan-
tastic rates of interest.[1] The United States Congress
appropriated $100,000 in 1820 to assist the American Coloni-
zation Society in its venture of returning negroes to Africa
from the United States. Not until 1944, however, did the
U.S. establish a full-fledged technical assistance mission in
Liberia.

However, it was in 1926 that the most dramatic single
event in Liberia's economic history took place. On October
2nd of that year, the Liberia Legislature approved a concession agreement with the Firestone Plantations Company.
Under the terms of this agreement, Firestone was granted
a 99 year lease on 1 million acres for the purpose of producing and processing natural rubber. The long-run effects
of this momentous move did not begin to materialize until
many years later. However, Liberia did receive an immediate benefit in the form of a loan from the Finance Corporation of America. a Firestone subsidiary created for just
this purpose. With the proceeds of this loan, the Government was able to retire its outstanding debts to European
lenders.

Thus, in 1940, Liberia had one major investor, a loan
payable to this investor, a customs receivership established
under the terms of the loan agreement, and little else--
except independence. But as valuable as independence was
to Liberia, it proved to be an asset which could not be
enjoyed without cost. Neighboring territories, as colonies
of European powers, were receiving relatively large
amounts of both private investment. Between 1870 and 1936,
public and private capital entering British West Africa
amounted to Ł 116.7 million of which Ł 50.9 million was
public and Ł 65.8 million was private. For the Belgian

Congo, the total foreign investment was £143.3 million of which £35.8 million was public and £107.5 was private. [2] The private investment in these countries provided employment, incomes, exports, and profits for reinvestment. The public capital was transformed into infrastructure investments such as roads, power, transportation, schools, and hospitals. Liberia's economy meanwhile languished because of a lack of foreign investment. The nation was too poor to provide needed capital from domestic sources, even if the savings of wealthy Liberians had all been invested domestically instead of abroad.

Under a treaty between the United States and Liberia, American troops were stationed in Liberia during World War II. American interest in Liberia was reawakened by this contact, with the result being the establishment of a United States Economic Aid program in 1944, and construction of the Port of Monrovia in 1946-1948. Shortly thereafter, the Government and the Liberia Mining Company concluded their concession agreement. This renewed inflow of foreign capital initially came almost exclusively from America. Gradually, however, other nations came to supply increasing amounts of aid and private investment. Nevertheless, the United States has remained the principal supplier of capital and technical assistance. Of more than $437 million of foreign private investment as of 1960, firms wholly owned by United States investors were responsible for $106 million or 24 per cent of the total. If LAMCO, which is financed primarily with United States capital, is included, the United States total becomes $321 million or 74 per cent of all major investments. This chapter will describe briefly a selected number of foreign firms currently operating in Liberia with particular emphasis on the motivations behind their decision to locate in this West African country. All of the firms discussed in this chapter are American. There are two reasons for this selection. These are, individually, the largest companies with one exception, and one of these is the oldest of all private businesses in Liberia. Furthermore, the details of the investment decision process are well documented for these United States firms, either in published volumes or through personal interviews by the author with the persons directly responsible for the investment.

BUSINESS MOTIVATIONS AND ECONOMIC THEORY

The models of business firms constructed by classical (and neo-classical) economists in America and Great Britain place the entrepreneur in a central, albeit a passive, role. This creature of economists has been analyzed primarily in terms of the functions which he performs. [3] In general, the most important motivation imputed to the entrepreneur by economists has been the desire for profit.

Entrepreneurial motives other than that of profit have been recognized by some classical economists. Marshall observed, for instance, that religion is a more intensive motive than economic gain. Since, however, most of a man's life is spent in economic pursuits, these activities do more to mold his character than do religious values. [4] Economists have also recognized the influence in particular instances of the motives of power, prestige, desire for growth, preference for security and the quiet life. These entrepreneurial drives have been generally admitted by the side door, however, and they have been applied most frequently to explanations of monopoly behavior. The competitive producer must, under the pressure of market forces, if not because of personal desire, give all thought to profits. [5]

Even Veblen, a critic of the methodology of "orthodox" economists, contructed a theory of the entrepreneur, in which the businessman was depicted as a promotor, seeking to earn promotion profits instead of producing useful goods and services. Veblen viewed the promotor as a saboteur of the productive mechanism, standing in opposition of the "engineers" who were assured to be driven by such motives as the "instinct of workmanship" and "parental bent." [6]

Neither the profit-seeking entrepreneur of classical economists nor the promotor of Vebelen provide an adequate basis for explaining many current economic problems. [7] In their study of underdeveloped countries in particular, economists have begun to show awareness recently of the importance of motives other than profit. The profit motive is not a general theory which has application to all societies. [8] A change in attitudes of people in underdeveloped countries toward economic gain is often as important to a solution of the problem of raising real income as a change in

the proportions of land, labor and capital used in production.
A similar awareness of the significance of business motivations other than for profit has appeared in the United States
in recent years.

A general theory of entrepreneurial behavior in capitalis-
tic economies has not yet been developed. Nevertheless,
tacit agreement seems to exist among serious students of
this problem that the profit motive of classical economic
theory is inadequate to explain and predict many aspects of
business activity. Moreover, the entrepreneur is not a
passive, atomistic creature who adjusts as best he can to
uncontrollable market forces, but a person actively engaged
in changing conditions to create, as best he can, the ideal
climate in which he may thrive. [10] A businessman exists and
acts within a framework of material and institutional limitations and social sanctions, among the latter being the climate
of ideas, or Zeitgeist of the whole society. He knows what
he can and cannot do within such limitations and, most significantly, often comes to conceive this social role as being
just what his society dictates it should be. For instance, the
businessman accepts the necessity to bargain collectively, to
donate in the proper amounts to charities, and to be neither
unresponsive to change nor too radical an innovator.

If this businessman undertakes foreign investment, he
will probably carry with him the same attitudinal and
response patterns which characterize his behavior in the
American economy. What motivates him to invest abroad
and how he views his role in the foreign economic system
will not only determine his conception of success and failure,
but will also determine the contribution which his investment
makes to the economic well-being of the people of the host
country.

THE PROFIT MOTIVE

Importance of Profit Motive

While the attitudes of American businessmen in Liberia
reflect the social and economic values of their country as
well as the investor's personal ethical predilections, it is
exceptional to discover one who will deny the primacy of the

profit motive as an explanation of his foreign operation. It
is very likely that profit is the prime cause of most American direct investment in Liberia, since profit as a goal cannot be ignored, if only because of the desire to avoid losses.
Even philanthropic organizations must show some kind of
"return" for the benefit of the donors to the project. But
having taken the necessary steps to produce an acceptable
pecuniary return, the entrepreneur is free not to slant every
decision in favor of profit. [11]

Profit and the Kind of Investment

Orthodox economic theory states that capital will flow
from areas of lower to those with higher net returns. In
equilibrium, the supply of capital will be so distributed
internationally that the marginal productivity of investment
is equal in all alternative uses, allowing for differences in
risk between countries. Even generally acknowledged
differences in investment risks, however, frequently are
not fully reflected in interest rates or in potential rates of
profit, a fact which may retard foreign investment,
especially in areas where risk elements are very great.

More important than the average rate of return as a
determinant of the volume of capital inflow into a country,
however, is the expected return of specific industries. In
fact, underdeveloped countries which may seem to offer the
greatest opportunities for the development of new markets
seem to be the least attractive to businesses catering to
domestic demands. In such countries, the principal form of
foreign investment is in "extractive", or export-oriented,
industries.

Various considerations determine the location of foreign
investment in export industries in underdeveloped countries.
First, the expansion in the demand for petroleum, iron ore,
and other raw materials since 1940 has led to increased
search for, and exploitation of, foreign sources of supply.
United States and Western European domestic reserves of
some products, such as iron ore, became greatly depleted
during and since World War II. The concomitant developments of reduced supply and increased demand for iron ore
in the industrial nations explain the reasons for the formation of such companies as the Liberian Mining Company in

1948, its financial success thus far, and the initiation of other iron ore mining companies in the period 1958 to 1963. Secondly, the internal markets for most products and services in underdeveloped countries are small. Investment in manufacturing, public utilities, trade and finance is thus retarded, in contrast with extractive operations which market the resultant products in highly industrialized countries.

Thirdly, foreign capital producing goods for domestic sale requires, if it is to be efficiently used, complementary investment in power, transport facilities, and other developmental and social capital projects. In underdeveloped countries, the necessary financial resources for developmental and social capital either do not exist or are not effectively mobilized.

Fourth, underdeveloped countries frequently are geographically quite different from the industrial countries where capital imports originate. Because of Liberia's absolute advantage in rubber production emanating from her climatic and soil endowments, it is not surprising that the first major American business investment in that country was in natural rubber production. Likewise, profit considerations were bound to bring iron ore mining to Liberia. Commercially exploitable ore was discovered in the mid-1930's in Liberia, when a Dutch concern conducted exploration of the Bomi Hills area. When it was discovered that the Dutch owners were merely a front for the actual German owners, a concession was not granted by Liberia. Private investment is occurring in Liberian timber production to utilize a rich resource of the country. These examples illustrate the tendency for foreign private capital, primarily because of profit considerations, to exploit the unique resources of Liberia, a tendency which invariably leads to exports of these resources to industrial countries.

Liberian Foreign Investment

The profit potentials of an investment abroad by an American business are greatly affected by the general political climate in the underdeveloped country, as well as by legislation and governmental policies relating to foreign investment. [12]

Liberia possesses a constitutional form of government, structured along the lines of the Federal Government in the United States. In practice, this government is controlled by a one-party political organization. It has, however, continuously espoused a foreign policy having as its cornerstone close alignment with the West.[13] President Tubman has unequivocally declared his desire to establish and maintain firm diplomatic, commercial, and spiritual ties with the government and people of the United States.[14] Many foreign businessmen in Liberia have asserted that this official policy along with the personal honesty of President Tubman, exerted a considerable influence upon their decision to establish a business in Liberia.

Since 1944, under the Tubman administration, the Liberian Government policy of the "Open Door" has encouraged private foreign investment. A restatement of this policy is found in almost every Annual Message of the President. For example, in 1952, President Tubman stated:

We shall continue to encourage foreign investments and the granting of foreign concessions in cases where Liberians have not reached the place where they are capable and competent to explore and exploit the potential resources of the country. We shall continue to guarantee protection to investors and concessions, however, it must be on the basis of mutuality.[15]

Private foreign investment in Liberia is also encouraged because of the monetary system of the country, which is based upon the American dollar. This fact has made it possible for the Country to follow a policy of permitting free foreign exchange transactions at a time when all other African countries operated under some sort of exchange control system. However, the absence of exchange controls has had, at best, only a slight effect upon American investors in that country. European business firms have been most attracted to Liberia because of its dollar currency.[16]

A major Liberian policy of importance to private foreign investors is the nature of concessions offered by the Liberian Government. A noticeable tightening of concession terms has taken place since 1945. The Liberia Mining Company concession, which originally allowed a royalty of $1.50 per ton of ore to the Government, has been revised to give Liberia a

share of profits. The Liberia-American Mineral Company
was required to give 50 per cent of its common stock to the
Republic of Liberia in its original concession in 1954. In
1957, an agreement between the Liberia Mining Company
and the Government to exploit ore deposits in Grand Cape
Mount County gave an equity interest of 50 per cent to the
Liberian Government, 35 per cent to private Liberians, and
15 per cent to the Liberian Mining Company. [17]

In a similar manner, agricultural concessions have
become more restrictive in recent years. The Firestone
concesssion signed in 1926 gave the company a ninety-nine
year lease on 1 million acres of land. Since 1945, there has
been a tendency for the size of concession areas to become
smaller and for the length of the concession period to
become shorter.

Foreign Business Attempts to Mold Political Systems

Participation, either overtly or behind the scenes, by
foreign businesses in the government of a country is now an
unknown practice. One of the more inoffensive methods
whereby a foreign investor may attempt to mold political and
economic affairs of the host country to his liking is through
financial assistance.

Liberian financial history presents a picture of a poor
country forced to borrow abroad from time to time, and
often not reaping the maximum possible benefits from such
loans because of onerous terms of the loans and because of a
failure to achieve a satisfactory level of financial and administrative competence. [18] When Harvey S. Firestone began
seriously to investigate Liberia in 1924 as a location for his
projected rubber plantation, he discovered a nation relatively deep in debt. The outstanding indebtedness at that
time consisted principally of $1.18 million due on a loan of
$1.7 million received in 1912 from a consortium of American,
French, British, and German bankers. [19] The remnants of a
multi-national Customs Receivership provided for in this
Loan Agreement, were administering the nation's fiscal
system. Because of the Firestone Company's aversion to
non-American control of rubber producing areas, it was
desired to have the Loan of 1912 replaced by one from an
entirely American source. Strongly supported by the United

States Department of State, Firestone and the Republic of
Liberia, negotiated a loan agreement to supplement the
Planting Agreement of 1926. The loan agreement provided
for the issue of up to $5 million in forty year 7 per cent
bonds by the Republic to be sold to the Finance Corporation
of America. [20] The Loan Agreement provided for appoint-
ment of an American Financial Advisor, who was given
broad policy-making as well as administrative powers. [21]
Among other things, the Financial Advisor was to receive
all revenues of the Liberian Government and take a first
claim upon them for interest and sinking fund requirements
imposed by the Loan.

The effects of the Loan of 1926 were, generally, favorable
to both the Firestone Company and the Liberian Government.
The latent possibility of European influence being exerted
upon Liberia was eliminated. Border attacks by the armed
forces of the colonial powers which ringed Liberia ceased
almost entirely after 1926. It is true that the economic
experiences of Liberia during the years when the Loan was
in effect were not all pleasant. Falling revenues after 1929
caused the Government to declare a moritorium on debt
service in 1931. As a result of this act, the United States
withdrew diplomatic recognition of Liberia until President
King was replaced by Edwin Barclay. Instead of reacting in
favor of the Firestone Company, the loan could very well
have been the reason for the company becoming a victim of
Liberian ultra-nationalism and expropriation. That such a
course of action was not followed was most fortunate since
foreign investments in later years were attracted to Liberia
partly because of the manner in which it handled this situation.

Interaction Between Foreign Investors

In many ways, the profitability of a given foreign business
in Liberia is affected by its relations with other foreign
investors. Firestone gave assistance to Goodrich in meeting
some of the technical problems of opening up a new rubber
plantation. The financial success of the Liberian Mining
Company indicated to the investors in Liberia-American
Minerals Company that iron ore could be profitably mined in
Liberia. Also, by observing the mistakes made by the

older company LAMCO officials were able to avoid certain costly pitfalls. Furthermore, a new investor may inherit a legacy of good or bad public opinion, depending on the actions of older companies. The linking by Liberians of prosperity since 1940 with rubber and Firestone, has eased the problem of gaining acceptance by other American businesses. At the same time, Goodrich managers reported that they encountered some resistance to recruiting labor, because of the circulation of stories of undesirable treatment of rubber workers at Firestone.

A foreign business may also exist for the express purpose of aiding other foreign businesses to locate in a country. The ill-fated original Liberia Company of Edward R. Stettinius was formed, primarily, for the purpose of acting as a catalyst to attract investment into Liberia from abroad. [22] The modus operandi of the company was to seek out potentially profitable investment projects. These would then be developed up to the point of actual investment, at which time it was hoped a private investor could be interested to undertake the venture. In some cases the company planned to finance the investment itself, expecting later to sell the business to private Liberians or to foreign interests. By demonstrating the profitability of particular enterprises, the Liberia Company hoped to attract $10 million of private investment into Liberia. [23]

Foreign private investment in Liberia has also been affected by the amount and type of United States public investment in that country. In particular, direct benefit has been gained from the Free Port of Monrovia, Roberts Field and highways. Indirect benefits accruing to private investors from education and health improvements have been considerable.

Firestone's Search for a New Supply of Rubber

Details of the Firestone search for a new source of supply of natural rubber are well described in several studies. [24] It is a story of resistance of one consumer to a system of price control imposed by foreign producers of a product. Following World War I, the over-expanded rubber industry of Southeast Asia was caught in a squeeze between high costs and declining world prices of rubber. After the failure of private rubber producers to control the marketing of rubber in order to raise prices, the British Parliament enacted the Rubber Plantation Act in 1922.

This legislation, popularly termed the Stevenson Plan, was
stated by Winston Churchill to be a means by which England
could pay her war debt to the United States. American
rubber goods manufacturers in 1922 accounted for about 70
per cent of world consumption of rubber. Because of this
obvious attempt to burden American rubber consumers with
the cost of maintaining the British producers, Mr. Firestone
rebelled. "I am going to fight this law with all of the
strength and vigor that is in me," he declared. "I do not
believe that for the benefit of a few stockholders, any
government has the moral right to make a law restricting
the output of a product of the soil so universally used as
rubber. " [25]

At first, Firestone stood almost alone in opposition to the
Stevenson Plan. He undertook a campaign designed to
arouse public opposition to the plan and to stimulate American interest in investing in rubber culture. "America should
grow its own rubber" became the slogan of this two-pronged
effort. [26]

Mr. Firestone's program to increase the output of
American-owned rubber was due to the importance he
attached to the role of the automotive industry in United
States prosperity. But of equal significance was the consideration which he attached to the importance of rubber to
national defense. America's dependence upon rubber grown
under a foreign flag, he argued, "is not only most serious
from a commercial point of view.... our War Department....
explained how serious would be our situation under present
conditions in time of an emergency. " [27]

The almost fanatical dedication of Mr. Firestone to the
cause of American-owned rubber plantations led him to
investigate the possibilities of establishing plantations in
Mexico, Sarawak, the Phillippines, and Liberia. From
these prospective sites, Liberia was selected by Mr. Firestone for the reasons that the country was politically independent, that it had a record of especially close relations
with the United States, and that rubber trees had been found
growing there which proved the suitability of Liberia to
rubber culture.

The activity of the Plantation Company during World War
II is alleged to be concrete evidence of the patriotic motive
of its founder. With the principal sources of rubber for the

United States cut off, because of enemy occupation of Southeast Asia, the Firestone Plantation in Liberia tapped its
trees at an accelerated rate. By this practice, rubber production was increased, but the life span of the trees was
drastically shortened. This practice, however, might con-
ceivably be explained on economic grounds just as well as by
patriotism.

HUMANITARIANISM

Stettinius Associates

Almost every private United States businessman in Liberia
states as one reason for his investment the desire to aid and
assist in the improvement of the health and education of the
people of that country. The Liberia Company, organized in
1948, had as a prime motive the alleviation of the social and
economic ills of Liberia. The organizer of the company was
Edward R. Stettinius, who as Secretary of State of the United
States, became aware of Liberia as an economically retarded
nation to which the United States owed a moral obligation to
assist. In 1945, Mr. Stettinius and others organized the
Stettinius Associates-Liberia, Incorporated, a corporation
having the purpose of investing, and stimulating others to
invest in Liberia. [28] The company signed a Statement of
Understanding with the Republic of Liberia in September,
1947, according to which:
1. The corporation was granted an eighty year concession
   to exploit any line of business, except activities
   already expressly granted to other concessionaires.
2. The Liberia Company was formed as a subsidiary of
   Stettinius Associates to promote business investment
   in Liberia.
3. The Liberia Foundation, a philanthropic trust was
   created for the purpose of financing public health and
   education programs, including scholarships to Liberians for foreign study.
4. The shares of stock in the Liberia Company were
   divided as follows:

Republic of Liberia   25 per cent

> Liberia Foundation   10 per cent
> Stettinius Associates   65 per cent

Although Stettinius Associates was a business venture
devoted to earning profit, the company possessed a strong
humanitarian bent. The policy of promoting the health and
education of Liberian citizens was embodied in the Statement of Understanding as a contractual obligation:

> It shall be a primary concern of the Liberia Company
> to advance the welfare of the people of Liberia, and
> the inauguration of every project shall be accompanied
> by provision for health and training of Liberians who
> are employees or prospective employees of the Liberia
> Company or any subsidiary thereof. [29]

Mr. Stettinius further emphasized the idealism underlying this venture when he stated, "With our techniques and
know-how, it just isn't necessary for them (Liberians) to
live poorly. I would not, personally, be doing this on a
purely commercial basis." [30]

Despite its "idealism," the Stettinius undertaking was a
bold business venture. Never before had such an all-
inclusive concession been granted by Liberia, and probably
never again will a similar agreement be made. Had this
company been successful, it had the potential power to control every foreign business investment entering Liberia
after 1948. While such complete control would have been
unlikely, even under the most propitious circumstances, a
reasonable degree of success by the Liberia Company would
have made it the dominant economic force in Liberia. President Tubman found it necessary to defend this concession
against critics who asserted that it virtually ceded to the
Liberia Company the development rights in all natural
resources. The President replied that the critics of the
Statement of Understanding had done little in the past to
develop the resources which they claimed Liberia possessed
in great abundance. He argued further that private business
financing of economic development was preferable to public
loans, that the Statement was not as liberal as the Liberia
Mining Company concession of 1946, that Liberia was founded
with United States private financial support, and that it must,
if it is to develop, use similar assistance. [31]

MISSIONARY MOTIVE

"Partnership with God"

In 1955, twenty-three mission groups were reported to be active, most of which were of American origin and support. [32] While some of the mission schools support agricultural activities and own property, they cannot be considered as business enterprises. There is, however, one American business firm, which has as its principal stated purpose the propagation of Christianity in Liberia. This is the firm of R. G. LeTourneau of Liberia, Inc., founded by Robert G. LeTourneau, of Texas, whose principal business activity is the production of earthmoving equipment. This dynamic personality, who assumed as the principal mission in his life the role of a Christian evangelist, made a pact with God in 1932, whereby he agreed to put ninety per cent of his personal earnings and a large block of company stock to the Lord's work through the LeTourneau Foundation. [33] In 1951, Mr. LeTourneau visited Liberia, and decided that the best way to teach the Gospel was by teaching basic American production skills to Liberians. [34] "Hungry natives will listen to us about God if we can show them a field of grain with a combine harvesting more in a day than they can eat in a year." [35]

An eighty year lease on up to 500,000 acres of developed land was obtained in 1952 for general agriculture, mining, and timbering operations. The Agreement further provides for a reinvestment of all of the profits of the company during its first five years of operation. In 1952, the first shipment of equipment to the concession site at Baffu Bay in Since County arrived, with $500,000 of earth-moving equipment, food for one year for the American staff, 500 New Testaments, and twelve "technical missionaries." [36] Since that date, the operation has been devoted to clearing bush with specially designed equipment and some planting of rice, fruits, and Nigerian oil palms. Of greater importance than these activities have been the Government construction contracts carried out by the company.

FOOTNOTES

1. See Brown, op. cit., for a detailed discussion of Liberian international financing prior to 1926. For example, in 1870 President E. J. Roye negotiated a ₤100,000 loan in London which with discounts and advance interest payments, netted Liberia less than ₤30,000.

2. Kimble, op. cit., II, 395.

3. Schmpeter's entrepreneur is most important in the role of innovator, the playing of which causes the businessman to spark economic progress. Professor Evans has suggested that the entrepreneur may also perform other functions such as manager and controller in addition to being an innovator. Each of these types of entrepreneurs has a different frame of reference from which he operates. The innovator attempts to maximize adventure, the manager desires security, and the controller looks for maximum power. G. H. Evans, "The Entrepreneur and Economic Theory," American Economic Review, (1949), p. 340.

4. A. Marshall, Principles of Economics (8th ed.; New York: The MacMillan Company, 1920), pp. 1-2.

5. One explanation of this apparently narrow-minded method followed by economists is that the profit motive permits the construction of models which may be manipulated to yield determinate solutions. Since other business motivations are not subject to empirical measurement, they cannot be handled with the same degree of mathematical precision as can the profit motive.

6. Veblen did not criticize the validity of the profit motive so much as he contended that this drive would not lead to the best use of productive resources. The reader is particularly referred to Veblen, The Theory of Business Enterprise (New York: Charles Scribner's and Sons, 1904), The Engineers and the Price System, (New York: The Viking Press, 1921), and "Why is Economics Not An Evolutionary Science," Quarterly Journal of Economics, III (1898), pp. 382-397 (reprinted in M. Lerner, The Portable Veblen, (New York:

The Viking Press, 1948), pp. 215-250.

7. C. A. Hickman and M. H. Kuhn, Individuals, Groups
and Economic Behavior (New York: The Dryden Press, Inc.,
1956), Chapters 1-3.

8. Ibid., pp. 80-81.

9. Two scholarly treatments of the nature of business
motivations are M. Lauterbach, Man, Money and Motives,
(Ithaca: Cornell University Press, 1954), and the Hickman
and Kuhn volume referred to above. Both of these volumes
contain bibliographies of recent studies of businessmen's
behavior in western countries. Attention may also be called
to the studies of entrepreneurial history reprinted in F. C.
Lane and J. C. Riemerams, Enterprise and Secular Change,
(Homewood, Ill.: Richard D. Irwin, Inc., 1953), Part I.

10. W. T. Easterbrook, "The Climate of Enterprise,"
American Economic Review, (1949), p. 327.

11. Observation of Kenneth Galbraith, noted in Hickman and
Kuhn, op. cit., pp. 60-61.

12. See United States Department of Commerce, Factors
Limiting United States Investment Abroad (Washington:
United States Government Printing Office, 1953), for a
review of such conditions affecting American private investment in all parts of the world.

13. See R. L. Buell, Liberia, (Philadelphia: University of
Pennsylvania Press, 1947), pp. 7, ff. , and Gunther,
Inside Africa, (New York: Harper and Bros., 1953), p. 850.

14. In a major foreign policy speech in 1956, Mr. Tubman
stated, "The government and people of Liberia irrevocably
and whole - heartedly identify themselves in spirit and action
with the free nations of the world. " Mr. Tubman held that
Liberia would not sell or barter its integrity, that "any
infantile flirtation with the powerful and implacable foes of
democracy and freedom for temporary gain may involve a
price fatal (to Liberia's) own independence and very

existence. " Speech reprinted in Liberian Age, March 12,
1956, pp. 6-7. Mr. Tubman's reference to flirtation with
foes of democracy related to offers of economic aid made by
Soviet representatives at his inauguration in January, 1956.
An overt offer of assistance from Poland was renounced in
March 1957, New York Times, March 10, 1957, p. 3.

15. William V. S. Tubman, Inaugural Address, (Monrovia)
January 7, 1952. The door, it appears, is only open to a
select group. See previous footnote.

16. With an eye toward European investors, Mr. John Mac
Rae, Commercial Advisor to the Republic of Liberia stated
in 1953, "Liberia might benefit by having a soft currency. "
A more desirable way to encourage European business
investment in Liberia would be to shift Liberian imports
from the United States to Europe.

17. Liberian Age, August 19, 1957, p. 2. This agreement
led to formation of NIOC with the Government of Liberia
financial participation. See Chapter III, pp. 3-4.

18. The details of the negotiations and aftermath of the
Loans of 1871 and 1912 as well as the abortive attempts to
negotiate loans from the United States in 1901 and 1919, are
well told and documented in the principal histories of Liberia.

19. An internal floating debt of more than $600,000 and an
obligation of $35,000 due to the United States of America
completed the list of Liberian debts in 1924.

20. The Finance Corporation of America was formed by
Firestone to make this loan, because of aversion by Liberian
officials to borrowing directly from a company to which they
had granted a production concession.

21. See W. C. Taylor, The Firestone Operations in Liberia
(Washington: National Planning Association, 1956), p. 99.

22. "Liberia: Into the Twentieth Century, " Business Week,
December 13, 1947, p. 114.

23. Ibid. , p. 112. A few of the specific investments planned
by the Liberia Company were a national bank, an organization to collect, grade, process and market agricultural
products, an importing-exporting company, and public works.
Several businesses were organized under the sponsorship of
the Company, including a hotel, a fishing and cold storage
company, an airline, and a trading company. It is perhaps
ironic that these businesses should be successful when the
enterprise whose purpose it was to attract private capital
should fail. Reliable sources gave as the reasons for the
demise of the original Liberia Company the expensive, top-
heavy management and the failure of the Company to obtain
an interest in the Liberia Mining Company. Following Mr.
Stettinius' death in 1950, the Company was reorganized on a
much smaller scale with only the profit motive in evidence.
Mr. Juan Tripp, president of Pan American Airways,
became president of the new Liberia Company

24. R. E. Anderson, Liberia, America's African Friend
(Chapel Hill: University of North Carolina Press, 1952),
Chapter 11;   Lief, The Firestone Story, (New York:
Whittlesey House, 1951); and Taylor, op. cit. , pp. 42-52.

25. Lief, op. cit. , p. 145.

26. For a discussion of the position of those opposed to the
Firestone policy, see C. R. Whittlesey, Government Control of
Crude Rubber , (Princeton: Princeton University Press, 1931),
p. 16.

27. H. S. Firestone, America Should Grow Its Own Rubber,
(Akron: May 15, 1923), p. 6.

28. Included on the Board of Stettinius Associates were
Philip D. Reed, Chairman of the Board of General Electric,
Ex-Under Secretary of State   Daniel C. Drew and Rear
Admiral William F. Halsey.

29. "Statement of Understanding between the Liberia
Company and the Republic of Liberia, " from Anderson, op.
cit. , p. 258.

30. "Idealism, Incorporated, Stettinius Associates," Time Magazine (50), October 6, 1947, p. 88.

31. Capping this list of positive reasons in support of the Statement of Understanding with Stettinius Associates, President Tubman noted that no surrender of sovereignty could compare to the 1935 amendment of the Firestone Planting Agreement when the company was given freedom from land rent and export taxes for ninety years. See W. V. S. Tubman, Fifth Annual Message, (Monrovia, 1948)

32. Cole, Liberian Yearbook, (London: The Diplomatic Press and Publishing Co., 1956), pp. 161-182.

33. "Partnership With God," Time Magazine, July 28, 1952, p. 65.

34. Loc. cit.

35. Ibid., p. 66.

36. Loc. cit.

The foregoing chapter has explored some of the motivations generating interest and investment by foreign firms in
Liberia with particular reference to American business
firms operating in Liberia. This chapter and the one which
follows will describe the principal operations of foreign
enterprises operating in Liberia, emphasizing the activities
performed by these businesses.

MAGNITUDE AND SOURCES OF FOREIGN INVESTMENT

Number of Foreign Investors

It is difficult to state with certainty the number of foreign
firms presently operating in Liberia since data covering both
outstanding concessions and those currently in active operation is incomplete. Furthermore, the concept of a "concession" in Liberian usage is a vague and flexible one. The
term at various times has been applied both to firms which
receive a monopoly right for the use and exploitation of a
natural resource such as a mineral deposit or an agricultural
advantage, and to commercial and manufacturing enterprises
which sign a specific agreement with the Liberian Government under which the firm receives tax and other concessions.
In 1961, the Bureau of Concessions listed more than forty
firms which had received approval by the Liberian Government and had signed agreements.[1] Some of these firms have
not yet become operative, and a few probably never will
begin production. In a few cases, the concessionaire
received only exploratory rights with the final agreement to
be negotiated when and if the firm becomes convinced by the
results of its explorations that the proposed operation would
be profitable. The Bank of Monrovia, in its 1960 Annual
Report, stated that twenty-five foreign firms were operative
in that year. This total evidently does not include the

hundreds of foreign-owned and managed retail establishments, some of which are major firms in Liberia.

A list of twenty-one selected concessions indicates that as
of January 1, 1962, the total investment of these firms
approximated $437 million. By principal industries, this
total was distributed as follows:[2] (Millions of Dollars)

Rubber and Other Agricultural Products	$ 49
Iron Ore Mining	382
Timbering	1. 3
Others	4. 3

While many firms are excluded from this total, they are,
on the average, small businesses which probably will not
add more than another $5 million to the total amount of
foreign investment in Liberia. It seems safe to employ the
figure of $445 million as the amount of foreign private busi-
ness investment in Liberia at the present time.

The dominant position of iron ore mining is readily
apparent from this summary. Of the $437 million of invest-
ment here recorded, iron ore mining accounts for 87 per
cent of the total. Furthermore, five companies have made
an aggregate investment of $414 million or 95 per cent of the
total. Of these five firms, four are mining companies and
one is a rubber plantation. This concentration, both in the
industrial structure and in the number of firms, plays an
important role in explaining the behavior of the Liberian
economy. [3]

Nationality of Foreign Capital

The principal source of the $445 million of foreign private
investment reported above is the United States, followed by
the Federal Republic of Germany and Sweden. The balance
consists of small amounts of investment which originated
from the Netherlands, Switzerland, Spain and England. In
addition, there is an undesignated amount of investment in
commercial enterprises, principally supplied by Lebanese.
Nationals, but also by English, German, French, Swiss and
Indian citizens.

One significant exception to the implied assertion that all
of this capital is from foreign sources must be noted. The

Table 5: Country of Origin of Principal Foreign Investments--
Liberia, 1962 (Millions of U. S. Dollars)

Country of Origin	Amount
United States	$ 106. 7 *
Federal Republic of Germany	105. 2
Switzerland	3. 5
Italy	2. 0
Netherlands	0. 7
Spain	0. 6
England	0. 6
Sweden	0. 5
U. S. - Sweden - Canada	215. 0
U. S. - Germany	2. 1
TOTAL	436. 9

*Includes $8, 500, 000 of Liberian Investment in the United
States controlled National Iron Ore Company.

Source: Office of National Planning, Annual Report, 1960-
1961, (Monrovia: 1961) and Office of National Planning, Annual
Report, 1961-1962, (Monrovia: 1962).

Liberian Government contributed $5 million to the capital of
the National Iron Ore Company in 1960, an amount equal to
one-half of the total equity capital of the company. [4] The
Government received an equivalent share of common stock
for this investment in lieu of the usual 50-50 profit sharing
arrangements with other mining enterprises. Thus, the
Government in this instance made a contribution to the

mineral deposit, as it did with the other companies, plus a contribution of equity capital. In return, the share of profits will be 50 per cent, reflecting the Government's capital contribution. This is the same share of profits it will receive from other companies to which the Government contributed only mineral exploitation rights. This $5 million of scarce capital funds which could have been utilized for education, roads, or public health was invested at a zero rate of return in iron ore mining.

A justification for this investment might be found in the fact that this particular deposit is not too favorably located, either for ease of ore extraction or of transportation; and therefore, the private investment would not have been undertaken in the absence of government equity participation which allows a sharing of the risk of development. There is no firm evidence that such was actually the case in this instance, but even if it were, the Government has available other fiscal measures such as tax holidays to induce private investment.

Fortunately, the amount of Government participation is comparatively small in this case, and the loss of alternate returns on the capital will not be critical. Nevertheless, a precedent was established which some feared would lead to larger, similarly financed investments in the future. The Office of National Planning strongly urged the Government not to establish this technique as a modus operandi in the future. In its discussion of the issue, the ONP noted that in some instances, Government equity participation in a private investment undertaking might be justified, as for example, if the development cost is substantial or if the enterprise requires government investment on grounds of national prestige; but it noted strongly that this procedure should not be allowed to become standard practice. "Among other undesirable features of such an arrangement," the ONP states, "the great danger is the tendency to abdication by Government of the sound and reasonable exercise of its powers." [5]

Given both the bargaining power of the Liberian Government due to possession of rich iron ore deposits, and her possession of other mining enterprises, there is, therefore, no practical or reasonable justification for financial participation in a business investment at this time.

Rate of Capital Inflow

Lacking regularly reported statistics on income and
financial transactions, it is not possible to document the
annual inflow of foreign capital to Liberia. Nevertheless,
examination of the economic history of the country reveals
that foreign investment has, for the most part, appeared in
a series of waves rather than as a steady flow. The Firestone investment was initiated in 1926, but it was not until
the period just prior to World War II that this enterprise was
really under way. The onslaught of the world depression in
the 1930's had stalled the development of the plantation for a
time so that regular production on a large scale basis did not
begin until the later years of that decade. Continued expansion and development of the plantation continued during the
war years which, coupled with rising employment as acreage progressively came into production, yielded the Liberian
Government and economy a modest but rising source of
income. On the heels of the close of the War, the United
States Government built the Free Port of Monrovia at a cost
of $20 million. As part of the same wave of capital inflow,
the Liberia Mining Company undertook the development of its
concession at Bomi Hills. The gestation period of this investment closed in the early 1950's. For the next few years, a
relatively small rate of capital formation in the form of roads
and a water system for Monrovia comprised the investment
inflow. B. F. Goodrich cleared its first acreage and planted
seedling rubber trees in 1955-1956, and firms such as
LeTourneau, the African Fruit Company, and the Liberia
Company began modest operations at about the same time.
No other investment of consequence was initiated until 1959
when the Liberia American Minerals Company commenced
the physical development of its concession. Comprising
almost one-half of all of the foreign investment in Liberia
and being concentrated within the space of four years, the
economic impact of the LAMCO investment was perhaps the
most dramatic single shock ever experienced by Liberia.
Wage employment increased, the money supply rose sharply,
and imports rose both as a result of the capital inflow and
as an induced result of rising incomes. Accompanying the
LAMCO capital inflow was induced investment in public construction, financed by pre-financing loans, and justified on

the basis of anticipated iron ore royalties. Inflation, concentrated in the personal service and real estate areas, was one of the manifestations of the rapid rise in national income. Real estate buying and residential and commercial construction vied with the iron ore mine for labor, and with the Government for the supply of loanable funds.

Supplementing the economic thrust generated by the Nimba investment were the developments of the Mano River and the Bong Mountain deposits between 1961 and 1964. By 1962, however, this rate of foreign investment had reached its peak and the annual inflow of capital declined in 1963 and fell even further in 1964. Government revenues declined as imports fell, and employment and personal income both experienced a similar slump.

Construction has also exhibited cyclical fluctuations which have heightened the instability of the economy since 1940. While total construction activity for 1961 is reported to be $23 million this figure represents construction contracts awarded in that year and not actual expenditures. Of this total, $18 million was for public building but less than $2 million was actually paid out in 1961. Furthermore, $16 million of this total was for the Executive Mansion and Law Courts Building. No new contracts of appreciable size were signed in 1962 and 1963, so by 1963, public building construction had virtually ceased; and this recession in building activity carried through until 1964. In that year, the receipt of foreign credits enabled work to begin on the Mount Coffee Hydro project. This upsurge in construction activity will be augmented by road, school building, and hospital construction in 1965-1967.

Primary road construction has also exhibited severe fluctuations since 1954. Between 1954 and 1960, 344 miles of primary road have been constructed at a total cost of $16.5 million. However, 1958 and 1960 saw the completion of 251 miles of the total with a value of $13 million. In all of these cases, foreign contractors held the prime contract with the Government. [6]

Thus, in 1964, the Liberian economy stood in a precarious position. The retardation of foreign investment was certainly not the sole cause of the recession in economic activity, since rubber prices fell at the same time, and construction activity virtually ceased. Nevertheless, the completion of iron ore

investment was a prime cause of the economic decline. This
experience serves to illustrate the nature of the instability
of an underdeveloped economy created by a primary reliance
upon foreign capital. When the inflow is steadily rising and
when it is sufficiently diversified both by industry and among
companies, the host country experiences a regular rise of
income. But when the inflow, because of its concentration
and lumpiness, appears in waves, as it has in Liberia, the
receiving country undergoes alternate periods of feast and
famine. Even if the long-term trend resulting from such an
investment experience is upward, this continual buffeting of
the economy by alternate surges of prosperity and recession
exerts a retarding effect on the long-term rate of growth. In
other words, had the same amount of investment been more
evenly spread over time and among industries, it is possible
that the resulting long-term growth rate would have been
higher than that realized so far.

PRODUCTION ACTIVITIES

Foreign private businesses in Liberia may be classified
according to whether they produce a product for export or for
domestic sale. The second group may in turn be subdivided
into manufacturing and service enterprises. While no particular method of classification is perfect in all respects, the
division of these firms into export and domestic industries
emphasizes the nature of the concession which the firm has
received, the disposition of its product, and the degree of
dependence of the investor on foreign markets.

It is impossible to obtain accurate and precise data of total
production of foreign business firms in Liberia for several
reasons. First, while the larger businesses do maintain
accurate records of the value of their principal product, they
often produce many services which are not priced in the free
market. For some of these services, the cost of production
may be taken as their value, although this measure may con-
ceivably understate the importance of the services to the
users. For such activities as hospitals, schools, roads, or
subsidized food and clothing, cost of production does not
reflect the use value of the marginal product, because of a
lack of competition in both the factor and product markets.

For example, a road on the Firestone Plantation contributes to the production of rubber, and its cost is presumably part of the price of the product. In addition, the same road yields services to Liberians and others, since it may be freely used for the transportation of merchandise and persons. Since the product in this case is free to the users, it is not possible to ascertain the value of the road to them; although its contribution in the form of external economies is apparent. A similar situation exists with other Firestone services, particularly hospitals and the services to local growers. Hospitals serve employed personnel, and as such, their cost is part of the production cost of rubber. However, hospital service is granted to families of local rubber planters, and the value of this service is not measurable. The cost of the hospital cannot be allocated between employee users and others, nor are there similar services available at an open market price, to use as a basis of estimating market value. Similar conditions also prevail for the Firestone services to local rubber growers. There is no way of estimating its value to the recipients from the cost of the service to Firestone.

Secondly, some services are rendered which may yield an economic value less than cost of production. For example, during the Presidential Inauguration in Liberia in 1956, Firestone made available to the Government a fleet of cars and a cadre of drivers and supervisors. The contribution of this service to the smooth conduct of the week-long ceremonies was considerable but indeterminate. It may have been worth less than the cost of the operation to Firestone.

Thirdly, some foreign businesses incorporated in Liberia both produce and market their product outside of Liberia and employ no Liberian resources. The only measure of production of these enterprises in terms of their contributions to the Liberian economy is in the form of taxes, fees, and royalties paid to the Liberian Government.

Finally, where production activities are susceptible to measurement, the fact is that they have not been recorded in many instances. Only recently has it seemed important to collect comprehensive economic data from all private business firms; however, the results have so far not been very productive of data.

Exports

Rubber

Rubber has been the most important product of Liberia
since 1940, giving way to iron ore only in the late 1950's as
the largest export commodity by value. One firm, the Firestone Plantations Company, accounts for the bulk of rubber
exports, and until recently was the only foreign rubber producer in Liberia having any amount of measurable exports.
Table 6 shows the record of this company from 1937 to 1963.
Output rose by more than three times between 1937 and 1941,
and increased again by more than two and one-half times
between 1941 and 1946. During the first of these periods, the
rapid growth of output is explained by new acreage coming
into production after the seven year gestation period for
rubber trees. Expansion of output during the war years is
partly explained by the same reason, but the company also
instituted the policy of "double tapping" trees to maximize
the contribution of the plantation toward meeting the severe
scarcity of natural rubber which existed at that time. Production by the company rose more gradually during the post-
war years, finally reaching its peak in 1958. In that year,
the Company began a long-range program of cutting old, low
yielding trees and replacing them with new, higher yielding
varieties. Under this program, 2,000 acres will be
replanted annually. Since a rubber tree does not begin to
yield any output until it is seven years old and reaches its
maximum yield point only after about twelve years, this
program will cause upwards of 14,000 acres to be non-
producing at the time the program reaches its peak. Thus,
the decline in output after 1958 will continue for some time
until the replanting cycle is completed. The new trees are
twice as productive as those being destroyed, so that the long-
run future for the company appears very favorable.
Other foreign plantations have not until very recently contributed more than a nominal amount to the total export of
rubber. In 1962, reported total output amounted to 97 million
pounds of which Firestone and Liberian planters accounted
for 94.2 million pounds. The unexplained difference of 3.8
million pounds, which is probably the output of other concessions, is less than 4 per cent of total exports for that

year. [7]

Table 6:   Rubber Acreage and Production--Firestone
           Plantations Company   1937-63

Year	Acreage (mature trees)	Production (000 pounds)
1937	15,850	5,211
1938	15,850	6,780
1939	30,042	10,684
1940	34,266	15,769
1941	36,042	18,290
1942	40,412	25,610
1943	45,661	33,149
1944	48,964	34,763
1945	55,668	41,242
1946	61,024	48,268
1947	66,181	46,669(a)
1948	72,009	47,747
1949	na	na
1950	na	na
1951	na	72,588
1952	na	72,707
1953	na	72,132
1954	na	75,000
1955	74,320	75,711
1956	na (b)	
1957	na	
1958	na	83,900
1959	na	83,000
1960	na	80,100
1961	na	79,600
1962	na	77,200
1963	na	77,700

(a) The rise in acreage and fall in production between 1946
and 1947 are accounted for by the cessation of double tapping of
trees which was practiced during World War II. For the
years 1938, 1940, 1941, 1943, 1946, 1948, and 1952 the
reported production exceeds the total export of rubber as

given in the Bureau of Statistics Foreign Trade Supplements.
The only explanation for this discrepancy seems to be that
the "years" in each case are not comparable, and that production and export do not always take place during the same
year. These explanations are not satisfactory. The trend,
however, is evident regardless of small discrepancies.

na - Not Available.

(b) While acreage of mature trees is not reported for the
period since 1956, it has declined because of replanting of
about 2,000 acres annually with higher yielding clones.

Source: 1937-1948, Meier, Economic Review of Liberia
        1951-1953, Firestone Tire and Rubber Company,
                   Annual Report, 1951, 1952, 1953, (Akron)
        1954   Cole, The Liberian Yearbook, 1956,
                   (Monrovia, 1956)
        1955   Firestone Tire and Rubber Company,
                   Historical Highlights of Firestone in
                   Liberia, (Monrovia: Oct. 1, 1955)
        1958-1963, Office of National Planning, Annual
                   Report, 1963-1964 (Monrovia: 1964)

Iron Ore

    The first shipment of iron ore from Liberia took place in
1951. During that year total exports of this commodity
amounted only to 55,500 long tons. By 1953, the Liberia
Mining Company was in full operation and produced 1.4 million tons. Production continued to expand, attaining a total
of 3.7 million tons by 1962. This output may be regarded as
the annual capacity of this mine. Beginning in 1961, small
quantities of ore were shipped from the NIOC deposit. In
1962, this company increased output slightly, but technical
difficulties restrained it from reaching its planned annual
output of 2.5 million tons as rapidly as had been expected.
LAMCO shipped its first production in May, 1963, and output
at Nimba has steadily risen since. Output for the first half-
year of operation was about 2.5 million tons. By 1968, with
all four mines in full operation, total iron ore exports will

have a gross value of $136 million. [8]

Table 7: Iron Ore Exports by Quantity and Value--
Liberia 1951-55 and 1959-63.

Year (a)	Quantity (000 of Long Tons)	Value (000 of Dollars)	Value per Ton (b)
1951	56	221	4.00
1952	665	3,071	4.52
1953	1,433	5,815	4.05
1954	1,239	4,365	3.51
1955	1,717	6,728	3.92
1956	1,407	na	na
1957	1,337	na	na
1958	1,510	na	na
1959	2,600	28,200	9.20
1960	2,900	34,600	11.20
1961	2,800	29,400	10.50
1962	3,700	32,400	8.66
1963	6,400	45,000	7.03

(a) Fiscal Years : 1951, 1952. Calendar years: 1953, 1954, 1955.

(b) The much higher unit price recorded for the later period reflects a change in the method of reporting value. For the earlier years, prices are F. O. B. Monrovia at cost, while for the period 1959 to 1963, values are delivered prices to the buyer.

Source: 1951-1955, American Embassy, Liberia, Annual Economic Review, (1952), and Republic of Liberia, Bureau of Statistics, Foreign Trade Supplement, (Monrovia, 1956). 1956-1958, United Nations, Economic Conditions in Africa Since 1950, (New York: 1959). 1959-1963, Office of National Planning, Annual Report, 1963-1964, (Monrovia: 1964).

Other Exports

The only other agricultural exports produced by foreign concessions are coffee and cocoa. Total exports of these

products are shown in Table 8. The amounts recorded are
inclusive of Liberian production as well as that of foreign
plantations. Information is not available on the production
of the latter group, except for 1960 when 41,000 pounds of
cocoa and 115,000 pounds of coffee were attributed to the
Liberia Company. These amounts are 1.9 and 5.7 per cent
respectively of total exports of each commodity in that year.

Diamonds were the third most important export by value
in 1963, having risen from less than $500,000 in 1953. Again
no data is available to permit measurement of foreign producers in this industry. While the largest firms are European, Liberians and other Africans work the deposits,
creating a chaotic condition in which smuggling and non-
reporting is rampant. Both the Department of the Interior
and the Bureau of Natural Resources and Surveys are continuously policing the concession areas to prevent poaching,
but officials of both of these departments admit that this
surveillance is only modestly effective at best.

Table 8: Cocoa and Coffee Exports--Liberia 1953-55
          and 1959-63

Year	Cocoa		Coffee	
	Quantity (000 of lbs.)	Value (000 of $)	Quantity (000 of lbs.)	Value (000 of $)
1953	596	149	909	247
1954	1,164	432	601	231
1955	1,059	315	736	227
1959	1,700	500	2,200	600
1960	2,200	500	2,000	500
1961	1,500	200	2,200	400
1962	1,800	200	4,200	600
1963	2,300	400	8,100	1,500

Source: 1953-1955, Bureau of Statistics, Republic of Liberia,
Foreign Trade Supplement, 1956 (Monrovia). Office of
National Planning, Annual Report, 1963-1964 (Monrovia: 1964).

Table 9: Diamond Exports--Liberia, 1953-63

Year	Value (Millions of Dollars)	Carats
1953	0.5	na
1954	0.5	na
1955	0.6	na
1956	2.4	na
1957	1.2	na
1958	2.3	na
1959	2.1	638
1960	2.3	967
1961	2.2	1,095
1962	4.5	854
1963	4.0	700

na - Not Available

Source: United States Department of Commerce, Liberia, A Market for U.S. Products, (Washington: 1965); Office of National Planning, Republic of Liberia, Annual Report, 1963-1964 (Monrovia: 1964).

Manufacturing and Construction

Foreign firms producing products for sale within Liberia are scattered and relatively little is known about most of them except that they exist. A sample of such firms reveals the output of such diversified products as soap, tiles, cement blocks, beer brewing, soft drink bottling, explosives, and oxygen and acetylene. Added to this list in 1964 was a rubber footwear plant, and the resumption of operation of a printing plant, jointly financed by the Liberian Development Corporation and foreign sources. The aggregate of production by all of these firms is reported to be small, but no statistics are yet available. [9]

Construction

Visible evidence of an active economy in any country is the

amount of construction under way. In Liberia, one continually
discovers evidence of construction activity in the form of
roads under construction, heavy and slow moving trucks
damaging laterite roads and slowing traffic, and piles of
sand and building blocks on the sidewalks.

While many small foreign and Liberian contractors operate in Liberia, the really large building jobs are contracted
to foreign firms. [10] While the precise amount of construction contracts awarded to foreign firms is uncertain, some
indication of it may be gleaned from the total of building and
road contracts. In 1961, it is reported that $23 million of
construction was undertaken in Liberia which amounted to 14
per cent of the Gross Domestic Money Income for that year,
almost all of which was performed by foreign firms. [11]

Service Industries

In response to the needs of a developing economy, hundreds
of foreign business firms have entered this country in order to
provide services demanded either by the Liberians or by the
large foreign enterprises described previously. In terms of
numbers, the traders dominate the picture of Liberia as a
country financed by foreign capital and organized by expatriate
entrepreneurs. Banking and transportation also are industries in which foreign businesses have been firmly ensconced
for many years. More recently, these older industries have
expanded their offering of services to new demands, and in
addition new types of enterprises such as engineering and consulting firms have made their appearance. The operation of
each of these industries, along with a description of the
services offered by some of the particular firms, will be presented to illustrate the role which these businesses have been
and currently are playing in Liberia.

Trade - Retail trade in Liberia is carried on by many small
and a few large firms, the latter generally also performing
wholesaling functions including importing, storage and
occassionally extension of credit. These firms are the back-
bone of Liberian trade and commerce except for rubber and
iron ore. They are centered in Monrovia but are also found
in almost every main village. Improved transportation has
greatly reduced the cost of hauling goods into the interior

where professional traders buy merchandise with money, and offer what is, to the primitive villager, an awesome variety of imported goods. The terms of trade between the villager and the trader reflect the strong monopoly-monopsony position of the latter. The trader purchases small quantities of rice, palm kernels or other products and ships a consolidated supply of these products to Monrovia for export or for local sale. In remote hinterland areas, only one or two traders intermittently visit the village, and reportedly exercise their monopsony power to the fullest. Frequently, what the native buys represents the product of "target labor," and he sells with the aim of acquiring a specified sum of money for a specified purpose. The seller will generally accept whatever price is offered, seeking only the desired sum and paying little attention to the real cost of producing the product. Because of this psychology on the part of the native seller, the professional buyer is frequently able to offer a very low price, which is just as frequently accepted. While many buyers may be found in larger towns, oligopolistic collusion produces the same monopsony effect as described above.

On the other hand, these traders have a monopoly advantage vis-a-vis the rural Liberians, either because of the former's small numbers or because of collusion between sellers in establishing prices. At the same time, the rural Liberians, because of their exposure to western consumption influences and their rising income, have developed a growing demand for widening varieties of goods. Village handicraft industry is unable to supply many of these goods, such as beer, cigarets, shot gun shells, and the omnipresent Coca-Cola. In other cases, locally manufactured goods cannot compete in quality with imported products. For all of these reasons, the trader is able to sell his imported merchandise at relatively high prices.

The large retail-wholesale firms import on their own account and maintain bonded warehouses at the Free Port of Monrovia. A few of these firms utilize local financing, but most of them have foreign credit arrangements. Those firms importing consumer durable goods such as automobiles maintain service facilities to supplement their commercial activities.

Virtually all of the small retail, and many of the

retail-wholesale businesses, are owned and operated by
Lebanese nationals. The Lebanese merchant is found in all
parts of West Africa, but his position in the Liberian
economy is stronger than anywhere else. In former British
and French colonies, mercantile functions were performed
by firms from the ruling country with the activities of other
nationals such as the Lebanese or Syrian occupying a marginal position in these economies. Because Liberia had no
"mother country" to gain a monopoly position in this area,
the void was filled by Lebanese and Syrian firms. Some of
the oldest of such firms have been in Liberia for more than
forty years. In addition to these businesses, there are to be
found German, English, French and Swiss commercial
establishments. The only American businesses of this sort
are the United States Trading Company and Tropical Trading
Company, subsidiaries of Firestone Plantations Company and
the Liberia Mining Company respectively.

A third type of sales enterprises may be briefly mentioned.
This is the number of sales and branch offices of foreign
manufacturers. These offices are usually one-man operations and employ only one or two Liberians each. Nevertheless, they supplement the large general stores, some of
which are agents for foreign producers of durable goods. It
may truly be said that anything can be bought in Liberia if the
buyer has the patience to ferret out the store which carries
what he wants and is willing to pay the price.

Banking - In 1955, three banking institutions were operative
in Liberia. Two of these banks offered general banking
services and the third provided, at that time, only limited
facilities. Since then, four other banks have been added to
the total.

The Bank of Monrovia, the oldest of these insititutions,
began operations in 1935, as a subsidiary of the Firestone
Plantations Company. It was designed to replace the branch
of the Bank of West Africa, which withdrew from Liberia in
1930. [12] The main office of the bank is located in Monrovia
with branches rendering service to Harbel, Robertsport,
Greenville, River Cess, Buchanan, and Harper through the
United States Trading Company and the Oost Afrikaanische
Compagne. The major services include loans, holding of
deposits accounts, foreign transfers and fiscal agent

functions for the Government of Liberia.

The Bank is the largest domestic creditor of the Government, holding $10 million of loans in 1962.[13] Other loans are to Liberians and foreign businesses. Under its present management, the Bank is expanding its loans to private Liberians adhering to a policy of credit rationing coupled with a fairly close adherence to the commercial loan theory of banking. Mortgage loans are not a major loan activity of the Bank, despite the Mortgage Guaranty Act of 1947, because of alleged large losses sustained by the Bank in the early 1950's. [14]

The Bank of Liberia was organized in 1954 as the Liberian Savings and Loan Corporation by a group of Liberians, with the express purpose of being "a Liberian Bank for Liberians." In 1955, the Bank reorganized under its present name, and received a credit of $2 million from the Swiss Liberian Finance Corporation. The Bank of Liberia had a slow start, with only about one hundred and fifty depositors before the reorganization and the acquisition of foreign credits. It has grown steadily since that time, and serves several outlying areas with a mobile banking unit which makes scheduled trips to interior towns, an innovation which carries out the initial purpose of the Bank--to "develop the idea of systematic savings by Liberians." [15]

The five other banking institutions are the International Trust Company, Tradevco Bank, Commercial Bank of Liberia, Chase Manhatten Bank, and the Union National Bank of Liberia. Of these, only the International Trust Company warrants special mention because of the unique service which it offers Liberia. The International Trust Company was organized in 1948 as a part of the Liberia Comapny, formed by Stettinius Associates-Liberia, Inc. It was later transferred to the World Development Corporation of Washington, of which it is still a subsidiary. In addition to regular banking activities, the ITC provides stock registration, transfer custody and trust services; and is an agent for United States and European insurance companies. However, its unique service is performed in its dual capacity as Maritime Administrator for the Republic of Liberia and as the statutory agent for foreign businesses incorporated in Liberia. Under the Maritime Registration Act, 1,122 ships with a gross tonnage of 11,945,593 tons were flying the

Liberian Flag in 1959, a fact which gives Liberia the third
largest registered tonnage of any country. From the fee
schedule of $1.20 per net ton upon registration and ten cents
per net ton each year, the Government has collected an average of $1.5 million per year between October 1955 and Sept-
ember 1960.

As of 1960, there were 1,217 foreign corporations taking
advantage of the Liberian Corporation Law. The principal
reason for foreign incorporation in Liberia is to take advantage of the country as a tax haven. Few of these businesses
maintain any operations in Liberia.[16]

Transportation - The most important transportation facility
in Liberia is the Free Port of Monrovia. This installation
was built with United States funds in 1946-1948; and although
it is operated by a private company, it remains the property
of the United States Government. Transfer of the Port to the
Government of Liberia is imminent, however. The details of
this investment are discussed in another chapter and will
not be repeated here. Two other modern ports currently are
in existence. The Buchanan Port was built by LAMCO as
part of its investment complex, and so far has been used
almost exclusively by this company. It is a general cargo
installation, however, and traffic is expected to increase
sharply in the near future. The third port was built by the
African Fruit Company at Since, but to date it has not been
extensively used either by this company or for general cargo.

In addition to shipping, international transportation is
provided by air from Roberts Field. This field was constructed
during World War II by the United States Army and later was
transferred to Liberia, who in turn granted operation rights
to Pan American Airways Corporation. PAA presently
manages the field, and along with the Government of Liberia,
is responsible for most of the investment in facilities.

Miscellaneous - The remaining foreign businesses in
Liberia cannot be conveniently classified and so are lumped
together in this final section describing the activities of
service industries. Included in this category are specialty
stores such as drug stores, individual professional persons
such as medical doctors, dentists, and accountants, and consulting firms particularly in the field of engineering. While

these enterprises and firms utilize virtually no capital and
hire few Liberians, their contribution to the Liberian
economy in helping to fill a vital gap in the high level manpower
supply is immeasurable.

EMPLOYMENT OF LIBERIANS

The total number of Liberians employed by foreign businesses in Liberia exceeded 50,000 in 1963. Firestone is the
largest single employer with a Liberian labor force of about
21,000. LAMCO ranks second with 12,000, but more than one-
half of this number were employed by contractors engaged in
the construction of roads, buildings, the railroad, and the
Buchanan port. When this construction ceases, the company
will employ only about 4,500 men. In 1963 a rising number of
unemployed workers appeared at both Nimba and Buchanan
because of the closing down of construction activity by LAMCO
and the problem became worse in 1964. Other contractors and
concessions are reported to have employed 10,000 men in 1963.
Unreported employment by foreign firms is estimated to be at
least 7,000, making a total of 50,000 jobs being provided by
foreign business firms. The total number of Liberians working in the money sector in 1963 is given as 90,000 of which the
Liberian Government employs 13,000.[17] This leaves 27,000
workers unaccounted for. Some of these are migrant and
part time employees, some are employed by private house-
holds, and some are in business for themselves.

INCOMES GENERATED

An estimate of the wage and salary payments by foreign
business firms along with other employers is given in Chapter
1 as $38 million. Other incomes generated by foreign enter-
prises within Liberia arise from their local purchases of
supplies, tax payments, and the stimulation of a Liberian
rubber industry. Each of these will be discussed below.

Local Purchases

In addition to direct personal incomes earned by employment in the American firms, Liberians also gain income

through purchases of locally produced products and services.

At one time, Firestone purchased millions of pounds of locally grown rice annually which it sold to its employees at a subsidized price of 2.5 cents a pound.[18] Other employers have also discovered that they must provide their workers with a regular supply of acceptable food if they are to recruit and hold a labor force. All of these, therefore, make local purchases of rice, vegetables, palm oil, fish, and other foods. In addition, other supplies and building materials are secured from the domestic economy. The total annual expenditure for this purpose is unknown; however, the net contribution which it makes to the Liberian economy is thought to be considerable. It should be noted that concessions are importing more and more of their rice in recent years because of a reputed decline in local production. If rice production efforts such as the Gbedin project are successful, it is expected that concessions will again turn to local markets for their purchases.

The very presence of expatriate personnel in conjunction with the operations of their business enterprises leads to a demand for the personal services of Liberians as household workers. No less than 1,500 Liberians are so employed, which at a monthly wage of $40 generates an annual flow of income in excess of $720,000.

Taxes and Royalties

All agricultural concessions granted by the Republic of Liberia stipulate a land rent of six cents per acre to be paid by the concessionaire. Agreements completed since 1940 permit the concessionaire to gradually develop acreage in the concession area, but rent must be paid on a minimum number of acres, whether developed or not. The B. F. Goodrich concession provides for rent payment on at least 50,000 acres beginning eighteen months from the date of the agreement.[19] LeTourneau of Liberia, Inc., must pay rent on at least 50,000 acres, beginning one year from the date of the agreement.[20] Similar provisions are found in other recent agricultural concessions by the Liberian Government.[21] Non-agricultural concessions impose an annual rent of six cents per acre on all land actually used, except that used for railroads, roads, ports, and airports.[22] The total income to the Liberian

Government from rental payments is not large. Both Goodrich and LeTourneau pay $3,000 a year each.[23]

Only Firestone, of all American business enterprises in Liberia, currently pays an income tax. In 1955, this payment amounted to about $4,500,000--about 85 per cent of total income tax receipts of the government. B. F. Goodrich and LeTourneau are likewise subject to income tax payments, although they have not yet earned taxable profits.

In lieu of income tax payments, mining and extractive firms pay royalties or have profit-sharing agreements with the Liberian Government. These profit-sharing arrangements may require as much as 50 per cent of the net profit of the firm being paid to the Liberian Government. This is twice the income tax rate applicable to agricultural enterprises. The original concession granted to Lansdell K. Christie by the Liberian Government provided for the payment of a royalty of five cents per ton plus "one per cent of the amount by which the average price in each year of one ton of pig iron exceeds 115 per cent of the average price for the ten year period ending with and including the year of shipment." Because of these terms this concession was regarded as extremely favorable to the company. It was reported in 1952 that the company's net profit varied between $7.00 and $12.00 per ton of ore shipped.[24] This report added that with an investment of about $10 million, and with production exceeding 1 million tons annually, the net profit at 1952 prices was between 70 and 180 per cent per year on total investment and between 170 and 400 per cent on the common stock. In the face of this unexpected rate of return, LMC and the Liberian Government renegotiated the concession agreement in 1952. The royalty was increased to $1.50 per ton for a five year period, with the Government thereafter to share in profits. The five year period preceding Liberian Government participation of profits was to permit the company to liquidate its bonded indebtedness and recover its investment in facilities. The effective date of profit participation was to be either April 1, 1957, or the date of liquidation of debt and recovery of investment, whichever was earlier. At such time, profits were to be shared according to the following schedule:[25]

1. Twenty-five per cent to the Government of Liberia for a period of five years.

2. Thirty-five per cent to the Government of Liberia for

the next ten years.

3. Fifty per cent to the Government of Liberia during
the balance of the period of the concession.

The profit-sharing arrangement went into effect in 1955,
the total income of the Government of Liberia from the
Liberia Mining Company amounting to $2 million in that year,
of which about one-half was profit-sharing at the 25 per cent
rate.

The LAMCO agreement, signed in 1953, provided for a
50-50 sharing of profits with the Liberian Government. Provision was also made for Liberian Government representa-
tion on the board of directors. This pattern is now taken as
the established policy of the Government for all mining
enterprises.

Table 10: Revenues by Major Source--Liberia, 1960
(Millions of Dollars)

	Dollars	Per Cent
Total Revenue	32. 3	100. 0
Concession taxes and Iron Ore		
Royalties	13. 3	41. 5
Other Income Taxes	1. 9	5. 9
Indirect Taxes	14. 5	44. 9
Others	2. 5	7. 7

Source: Bureau of Economic Research and Statistics, Annual
Report, 1960-1961, (Monrovia: 1961).

In addition to taxes on corporate profits and profit-sharing,
fees are paid by foreign businesses incorporated in Liberia
and by foreign ships operating under Liberian Registry.
Foreign personnel employed in Liberia, except those with
diplomatic status or presently under agreements of understanding between Liberian and foreign governments or the
United Nations, pay personal income taxes, as well as customs duties and other fees and local taxes.

Liberian Rubber Producers

The present local rubber buying program of Firestone was instituted in 1943. Prior to that time, only a few independent Liberian rubber plantations were operative, and they sold their output through Firestone under special arrangement with the Company. With the formalizing of the Rubber Purchase Program, Firestone began large-scale distribution of special clones which it had developed for use by small farmers. In addition, the company provided free advice on farm operations to a planter, and made available at cost the necessary buckets, cups, knives, and other tools required for rubber production.

By 1955, more than 4.5 million clones had been given to more than 700 Liberians. Gross sales by Liberian producers amounted to $2 million in that same year. By 1961, the total acreage planted in rubber by Liberians exceeded that of Firestone, although a considerable percentage was immature rubber. Aggregate production in 1960 totaled 15 million pounds having a gross value of $4.7 million. [26] Not all of these farmers received their trees from Firestone. Other concessions and the National Production Council have also distributed thousands of clones. Nevertheless, Firestone has the reputation for having initiated the industry and remains the principal buyer, processor, and exporter of "local rubber."

There are both economic and political advantages in Firestone's favor by supporting this program. The processing of Liberian rubber permits the company to utilize its plant at a higher and more constant level of operation than it otherwise would. The political advantage lies in the fact that a large and growing number of Liberians, including most of the "elite," have become directly involved in the continued presence and success of the Firestone operation in Liberia.

FOOTNOTES

1. Cole, Liberian Yearbook, 1962, p. 93-95.

2. Office of National Planning, Republic of Liberia, Annual Report, 1961-1962, (Monrovia: 1962), p. 32.

3. See pp. 68-70.

4. Office of Nationa Planning, Republic of Liberia, Annual Report, 1961-1962, (Monrovia: 1962), p. 55.

5. Ibid. , pp. 55-56.

6. Ibid. , p. 21.

7. The Liberian rubber industry is discussed on p. 87.

8. See Table 3, p. 30.

9. The writer, while working with the Office of National Planning, assisted in the preparation of an "Establishment Census. " The returns were quite scattered and so inconclusive that they have not been published.

10. Two of the three largest construction firms are Italian and the other one is Israeli owned.

11. Office of National Planning, Republic of Liberia, Annual Report, 1961-1962, (Monrovia: 1962), pp. 25-28.

12. Two employees of the Bank of West Africa died of yellow fever in 1930, and the Bank notified the Liberian Government that since this indicated a lack of improvement in sanitary and public health conditions, the Bank would be closed as of October 31, 1930. Charles D. B. King, Annual Message, 1930, (Monrovia), p. 22. Between 1930 and 1935, limited banking facilities were provided by the United States Trading Company, also a Firestone subsidiary. In 1955, the Bank of Monrovia was formed by the International Banking Corporation, a subsidiary of National City Bank of New York, which purchased the Firestone interest in the Bank of Monrovia.

13. Office of National Planning, Republic of Liberia, Annual Report, 1961-1962, (Monrivia: 1962), p. 19. This amount accounted for 11. 6 per cent of the total debt, domestic and foreign, of the Government at that time.

14. Republic of Liberia, Treasury Department, Report of the

Treasury Department, (Monrovia: November 14, 1952), p. 24.

15. "An Act to Create the Liberian Saving and Loan Corporation, " in Republic of Liberia, Department of State, Acts Passed by the Legislature of the Repbulic of Liberia During the Session 1953-1954, (Monrovia: Government Printing Office, 1954), pp. 48-57.

16. See The Journal of Commerce, December 29, 1955, p. 16 for a discussion of typical reasons for Liberian incorporation.

17. Office of National Planning, Republic of Liberia, Annual Report, 1963-1964, (Monrovia: 1964), p. 11.

18. This price compares to a market price ranging between 6 and 11 cents a pound in recent years. Firestone purchases in 1952, 1953, and 1954 of Liberian-grown rice amounted to 10. 6 million pounds, 5. 0 million and 0. 4 million pounds respectively. The decline in these purchases represents a shift to buying imported rice, not a decline in total purchases. W. V. S. Tubman, Annual Message, 1955, (Monrovia: 1955), p. 12.

19. "Concession Agreement Between the Republic of Liberia and the B. F. Goodrich Company, " (Monrovia: July 9, 1954), Art. IV.

20. "Statement of Understanding Between the Government of the Republic of Liberia and R. G. LeTourneau, " (Monrovia: January 18, 1952), Sect. 2. (Reprinted in Acts Passed by the Legislature of the Republic of Liberia During the Session 1951-1952, (Monrovia: Government Printing Office, 1952), pp. 8-15).

21. "Statement of Understanding Between the Government of the Republic of Liberia and the Afrikanische Frucht-Compangie Laeise and Company, " (Monrovia: July, 1953), Sect. 1. (Reprinted in Acts Passed by the Legislature of the Republic of Liberia During the Session 1952-1953, (Monrovia: Government Printing Office, 1953), pp. 91-98).

22. "Concession Agreement Between the Government of the
Republic of Liberia and the United African-American
Corporation, " (Monrovia: September 9, 1953), Art. 17.
(Reprinted in Acts Passed by the Legislature of the Republic
of Liberia during the Session 1953-1954, (Monrovia: Govern-
ment Printing Office, 1954), pp. 2-10.)

23. Firestone agreed to pay a rental of six cents per acre
on developed land in the Planting Agreement of 1926. In 1935,
however, an amendment of this agreement permitted the
Liberian Government to cancel $400, 000 of bonds issued
under the Loan Agreement of 1926 as prepayment of rent on
110, 000 acres for a period of ninety years.

24. Steadman, Report on the Fiscal System of Liberia,
(Monrovia: 1952), p. C-4.

25. "An Act Approving the Collateral Agreement Between
the Government of the Republic of Liberia and the Liberia
Mining Company, " (Monrovia: March 12, 1952), (Reprinted
in Acts Passed by the Legislature of the Republic of Liberia
During the Session 1952-1953, (Monrovia: Government Printing
Office, 1953), pp. 24-32.)
     This same agreement placed three Liberians on the
Board of Directors of the Company, a policy to which the
United States State Department objected. See United States
Department of State, Introductory Statement Regarding
Liberia Mining Company Negotiation, (mimeographed), 1952.
     The agreement also reduced, although it did not com-
pletely eliminate, the share of output sold to Republic Steel
Corporation at a preferential price, under an agreement
dated June 1, 1949. The original agreement permitted the
Republic to purchase 600, 000 tons of ore per year at $4. 67.
Continuation of this policy would have siphoned off a considerable amount of the Mining Company's profits, and would
have defeated the entire Liberian proposal to share in the
company's profits.

26. This section relies heavily upon data in Office of National
Planning, Annual Report, 1960-1961, Appendix A, Office of
National Planning, Annual Report, 1963-1964, (Monrovia: 1964),
and Taylor, op. cit., pp. 94-95.

CHAPTER 4   FOREIGN BUSINESS AND LABOR

In Chapter 1, the approximate size of the labor force in Liberia was discussed. The regional distribution and the mobility of labor, as well as the response of Liberian labor to various incentives, were likewise described. This chapter treats the special problems facing foreign employers in Liberia who seek to recruit and manage an indigenous labor force. Particular attention is given to the matter of labor productivity, inasmuch as labor is one of the two primary factors of production locally available to American employers. The particular significance of the productivity of labor lies in its role in determining income distribution. The pattern of income distribution resulting from foreign business operations in a country has been, historically, a matter fraught with both political and economic implications.

RECRUITMENT

Since almost all Liberian labor hired by foreign businesses is of unskilled or semi-skilled types, the discussion of recruitment is confined to problems of locating and hiring these groups of workers.[1] The principal source of unskilled labor is the native villages, and it is the village dweller who poses continuous difficulties to the employer.

The Carrot and the Stick Approach to Recruitment

Inducing workers to leave their villages to work on plantations or at other large installations, involves a compromise between the "carrot" and the "stick" methods of inducing labor movement. The stick approach--or the use of force-- is not, to the African, as undemocratic as a person reared in western world society may believe. This is so because the African native has never really been free from some type or other of imposed force. First of all, the physical

and natural conditions under which he lives place the native
under constant pressure to seek food, clothing, and shelter
merely to survive. In addition to these elemental factors
dictating the African's attitudes and mode of living are
psychological urges of prestige and emulation, which lead
him to produce in order to obtain the desired goods. In a
different manner, political or social forces continuously
operate to induce productive activity by the natives--or
rural Liberians. The tribal practice of "pawning, " whereby
one person is placed in servitude to another as a means of
settling an obligation, has been illegal since 1931.[2] Shortly
after pawns were "freed, " it was noted that instead of
responding to their new-found right to work for themselves
by working harder, they preferred to be idle. This reaction
has been interpreted as a phenomenon resulting from the
removal of force, whereby the former pawn, receiving the
freedom not to work as well as to work as he pleased,
chose to exercise the former privilege.[3]

Positive economic pressure imposed from outside of the
tribal culture, but which affects the tribal members' choices
of economic activity, comes from hut taxes. Designed as a
means of inducing certain kinds of economic activity on the
part of natives, the hut tax is preferable to direct control of
labor in that it allows the individual a range of free choice
as to how he desires to earn money to pay this tax. At the
same time, the hut tax directly affects recruitment of labor
by private employers, because the wage inducement they
offer possesses a higher degree of certainty of earning
money than most of the other economic activities open to
the worker.

Firestone Recruiting Methods

Private employers find it necessary to adapt their recruitment efforts to the tribal power structure, at the top of
which is the chief. By custom and by national law, this per-
sonage exercises broad powers of control over the disposition of the labor supply within his particular domain. The
recruiting methods followed by Firestone show how the
incentives of wage income offered by the company, combined
with the tribal political structure and with the national
Government of Liberia, enabled the company to assemble

effectively a labor force of 20, 000 to 30, 000 workers with a minimum of cultural and economic disturbance.

Because Firestone has discovered that it cannot rely upon voluntary job seekers to fill the labor requirements, the company has, by arrangement with the Department of the Interior, assigned to each Chiefdom a quota of men to be recruited for work on the plantation. For filling his quota, each chief is paid a bonus of fifteen cents per man per month during the months of January through June, and ten cents per man per month during July through December. [4] The number of workers covered by the quotas is less than the entire labor requirement of Firestone. For example, in January of 1956, the quota in effect amounted to 15, 100 men, although the aggregate labor requirement exceeded 20, 000. [5]

A number of factors are considered in setting the exact size of labor quotas. Among these are the number of able-bodied men in the community, the alternate economic opportunities available, and the extent of community development in the area. After the Company assigns quotas, the Department of the Interior must approve the distribution. Once the Government has placed its stamp of approval on an assignment, the Department of Interior, working through the District Commissioner in the area, assists the Firestone recruiter in meeting with chiefs, ironing out misunderstandings, and at times bringing official pressure on a recalcitrant paramount chief. The particular men assigned to work at Firestone are chosen by the chief. Some chiefs choose to allow men to remain away as long as they wish. Other chiefs prefer to rotate the workers on the assignment every three or six months. Firestone trucks transport workers to the plantation where they are assigned to a division. From this point, the hold of the company on unclassified, or unskilled, labor is extremely loose. Should the worker choose to leave the plantation the next day, possibly to go to Monrovia or to seek work elsewhere, he is free to do so. The only penalty invoked is the non-payment of the bonus to his chief. In this way, the responsibility is placed directly upon the chiefs, who, with their traditional control over village labor use, are free to cooperate or not, with a personal economic loss for non-cooperation.

The recruiting system described above generates a close personal relationship between officials of Firestone, the

Liberian Government and each village. Firestone recruiting
agents constantly tour the country, attempting to meet the
company's labor requirements by hiring individuals directly
as much as possible. It is necessary that the company agents
create and maintain a favorable opinion of themselves and
of the company among village chiefs and elders whose
cooperation is vital to the successful operation of the enterprise. One of the principal tasks of the General Manager of
the Goodrich Plantation has been to tour the surrounding
area in order to establish the necessary favorable rapport
with chiefs and elders. [6]

Recruiting by Other Employers

Not all foreign employers in Liberia find it necessary to
resort to the elaborate quota system of obtaining labor. It is
principally the plantations, with a relatively large labor
requirement, which must employ this method of labor recruitment. While B. F. Goodrich, during the spring of 1956, was
experiencing extreme difficulty in obtaining a labor force of
four hundred men, the Liberian Mining Company, a few miles
from the center of the Goodrich plantation, employed about
eighteen hundred Liberians. Officials of the mining company
reported that the Company averaged about ten applicants for
each job opening. [7] The Director of the Port of Monrovia
stated that only word of mouth notice was sufficient to elicit
all of the labor required by this installation. Each headman
employed at the Port maintains a following from which he is
able to draw when the call goes out for additional men. A
similar situation was found to exist with other iron mines
and with construction firms. In general, it may be stated
that mining, construction, and similar enterprises have
experienced, so far, little difficulty in locating and hiring
unskilled and semi-skilled labor, compared to the labor
recruiting problems of agricultural employers.

Labor Turnover

One labor problem related to that of recruitment, and one
with which almost all employers must contend, is a high rate
of labor turnover, especially among unskilled workers.
This problem has persistently plagued Firestone officials

since the company first hired labor in 1926. While the turnover rate in 1955 was reported to be lower than in previous
years, it still exceeded 30 per cent annually. [8] However,
field workers, among whom the turnover problem is most
acute, frequently leave their jobs for short spells, returning
again to the plantation. In recent years, only about 20 per
cent of the newly employed unskilled workers by Firestone
had never before worked for the company. [9] The Liberia
Mining Company reported a turnover rate of 4 per cent for
the month of February, 1956. [10] Officials of this Company
assert that February is a month with an unusually high turnover rate, since those workers who leave annually to cut a
farm, most often do so during this month. With the expansion
of the economy and the creation of new sources of employment, turnover at the mines has risen from this figure, but
it is below the rate for plantations.

Several reasons account for the frequency of workers
leaving and returning to a job, the most important of which
are the following:

1. The desires, or pressures upon a person, to return to
   his village to "make a farm" each year.
2. The fact that employment is sought in the first place
   to obtain money to purchase specific commodities, pay
   for a wife, or to pay taxes. When the required sum of
   money is accumulated, the worker leaves the job,
   until another economic target again compels him to
   seek employment for wages.
3. The spirit of adventure, or the desire to be with a
   friend may lead an individual to desert his present job
   and take another one.
4. A negative factor causing some workers to leave wage
   employment as soon as they become financially able to
   do so, is the unattractive living conditions which the
   workers find at their jobs. The term "unattractive" is
   purely relative, inasmuch as most employers provide
   what by western standards are living conditions superior
   to those found in the typical native village. Yet, simple
   mistakes or oversights by the employer make a big
   difference at times. Huts arranged in a row may vio-
   late the aesthetic sense of those who are accustomed to
   huts grouped in a circle or scattered at random.
   Others find residence with people of mixed tribal

origins less preferable than living in homogeneous
tribal groupings. Employers who encourage family
settlements, therefore, have been able to hold workers
better than those who do not. However, even when the
employer actively encourages such settlement, the
response may be poor, because of the attachment of
workers not only to their family, but also to their
village and to the tribal lands. [11] In such cases,
employers located near the workers' home village
appear to have some advantage in holding workers,
compared with employers such as Firestone, where the
place of work is often several miles from the nearest
village.

Freedom of the Individual Worker

A further important consideration in evaluating labor
recruitment in Liberia is the matter of the individual worker's
freedom of contract. Workers do not have to register with
the Government, nor do employers need to obtain Government
permission to employ specific persons. This policy of a free
labor force was instituted by Firestone in 1926. A letter from
Harvey S. Firestone, Sr. to President Charles D. B. King
in that year stated, inter alia [12]

The Company may employ any labor or laborers which the
Company may recruit or which may present themselves to
the Company at any of its operations or offices for employment, without such labor being first required to obtain
permission of, or be registered by, the Government.

Such labor so employed shall be free to bargain for its
terms and conditions of employment with the Company and
shall be free to sever its employment with the Company at
its own will and convenience.

We desire to point out to the Government again that the
success of our development in Liberia is largely dependent
upon the organization of a permanent and contented labor
force. This can only be done through free and unrestricted
employment and upon terms and conditions which are
agreeable to the laborers themselves.

We also desire to inform the Government that its repre-
sentations regarding labor presented at past conferences
received our utmost consideration and the interpretations
suggested herein are put forward in a spirit of cooperation
and in accord with the Government's problems.

In addition to following the labor policies set forth above,
the employer must pay wages directly to the workers.   In
times past, payment was frequently made to a third party,
often to the clan or paramount chief, with the worker often
receiving little or no part of his earnings for himself.   A
worker may still "contribute" part of his earnings to the
village treasury, but he is paid his full salary.   Nothing is
paid for him to a third person. [13]

WAGES AND HOURS

Labor Legislation

The foreign employer in Liberia has few legal requirements to meet regarding his employees.   The principal statutory limitations upon the employer relate to wages and hours.
Little of the protective legislation so common in western
industrial democracies exists in Liberia.

The organic labor law in Liberia is the Workman's Compensation and Protection Act of January 29, 1943.   This law
covers almost all Liberian labor employed by Liberian or
foreign firms.   Excluded from coverage by the Act are
nurses, Government employees, domestics and persons
earning more than $100 per month.   In addition to providing
for minimum wage and maximum hours, the Act also provides for the employment of non-Liberian labor.   Foreigners
are permitted to be employed in administrative, supervisory
or technical capacities.   For other jobs, Liberians are to be
hired, unless it can be shown by the employer that a shortage of the desired type of labor exists in Liberia.   The Act
contains no provisions regarding the minimum age of
employees, nor special rules governing the employment of
women and children or the employment of Liberians in haz-
ardous or fatiguing occupations.   Compensation must be paid
for injuries not caused by the worker's own negligence or

carelessness.[14]

Wages

The minimum wage since 1963 has stood at eight cents per hour for agricultural workers and fifteen cents per hour for non-agricultural workers. There is no legal minimum wage for skilled labor; however, Minimum Wage Committees are appointed in each county and district, whose function is to determine minimum wages for skilled labor. At one time these Committees functioned effectively in their capacity, but recent increases in wage and salary scales as a result of a rising labor demand have caused the de facto abolition of the Committees, despite their continued de jure existence. The Committees also determine the changes in the cost of living in each area, and adjust the minimum wage, provided a change of 10 per cent or more has occured in the price of goods commonly purchased by workers between January 1 of one year and the same date of the next.

The reader is referred to Appendix 5 where a lengthy body of wage data for both Liberia and other West African countries are summarized. By 1964, the minimum daily cash wage in agriculture was eight cents an hour; however, at Firestone and at other large plantations, the effective minimum wage was sixty-four cents per day despite the fact that a typical rubber tapper worked only about six hours daily. In contrast, the minimum wage in manufacturing of fifteen cents per hour was rarely paid except in construction, partly because most jobs in manufacturing are classified as semi-skilled or skillled. Semi-skilled mining workers received between twenty-five and thirty-five cents an hour while the minimum wage paid skilled workers was fifty cents an hour. Monrovia business establishments paid $60 per month for clerks and $250 per month for section heads.

Moreover, wages have been rising in Liberia, as indicated by the contrast between wage rates for selected occupations in 1953 and 1964. Within this sample, the ten year increase has been between 60 and 400 per cent. This coincides with the claim of Monrovia businessmen that in recent years, the annual rate of wage increases has averaged about 7. 5 per cent. This relatively rapid rate of wage increase is part of a general trend appearing in Sub-Sahara Africa which is

attributed to increased strength of labor unions, the necessity
to induce higher productivity and overcome the value of
leisure, the legal fixing of minimum wages by independent
countries, and the increasing demand for fringe benefits by
African workers.

Table 11: Wage Rates in Selected Occupations--Liberia,
1953-64.

Occupation	Wage 1953	1964	Percentage Increase
Rubber Tapper	.25/day	.64/day	156
Mining:			
Unskilled	.04-.05/hour	.25-.35/hour	400
Skilled	.16-.32/hour	.50 minimum	113
Construction:			
Unskilled	.05-.10/hour	.15/hour	100
Commerce & Banking:			
Messenger	$15/month	$25/month	60
Clerk		$60-90/month	
Typist		$75-80/month	
Stenographer		$150-180/month	
Teller		$100-120/month	
Department Head		$200-250/month	
Government:			
Typist	$60-100/month	$75-125/month	25
Messenger	$12-15/month	$25/month	100

Source: Appendix 5. 1964, U. S. Department of Commerce,
A Market for U. S. Products in Liberia, (Washington: United
States Government Printing Office, 1965).

Supply and demand forces partly explain the pattern of
wage increases in Liberia over the past ten years, especially
for semi-skilled and skilled workers. Expanding employment opportunities have created a shortage of Liberian labor
with demanded skills. While there is no official pressure to
employ Liberians in skilled jobs, employers have done so
wherever possible in order to reduce costs. Nevertheless,

the supply of skilled workers falls far short of the current
demand, and the gap is filled partly by use of expatriate
labor and partly by wage competition among employers.
Parodoxically, it appears from Table 11 that the largest wage
increases have been for unskilled labor. This follows a
historical trend, evident even in the interior, but which has
become more accentuated in recent years. This development can only be partly explained by market forces, inasmuch as a considerable, although unmeasured, amount of
unemployment of such labor now exists in Monrovia and
other urban centers. The best explanation of the disproportionate increase of unskilled labor wage rates is that Government policy has been able to raise minimum wages at a
faster rate than market forces would have done.

In addition to legislating a general rise in the minimum
wage, the Government has distinguished between agricultural
and industrial workers in the last two minimum wage laws.
In both cases, the minimum for industrial workers has been
higher than for agricultural workers--by 40 per cent in 1961
and 87 per cent in 1964. Two conflicting forces have been
exerted on legislators in their determination of minimum
wage policy. One is the demand for unskilled labor by construction and mining concerns upon whose activity the
economic future of the country heavily rests, which would
explain a larger differential between agricultural and industrial minimum wages. The other force is the cost-price
squeeze in which rubber producers find themselves. A low
wage is obviously a more desirable condition when selling
prices are declining. The upshot of this attempt to serve
both masters has been satisfactory as far as industrial
employers of unskilled labor is concerned, although there is
reason to suspect that the very nature of the jobs would have
served to attract sufficient labor to these employers even in
the absence of a favorable wage differential. At the same
time, rubber producers find that their wage costs have
risen while the shortage of tapper labor remains as serious
as ever.

It has been alleged that in the past wages of unskilled
workers were administered by tacit collusion between large
plantations and Liberian employers. Certainly the conditions
which would prompt such collusion have been, and still are,
present especially in rubber farming where the average

Liberian farm yield is less than one-third that of the largest
producer. Nevertheless, evidence to support this thesis is
almost impossible to accumulate. Moreover, whatever the
degree of collusion in the past, the present wage level for
tappers has caused many farmers to become marginal or
submarginal. Recent Government policy regarding minimum
wages has not reacted to the benefit of rubber producers,
whatever the reason for the increase.

Liberian wage developments reflect a combination of
market forces, legally administered wage rates, and possible
employer collusion. With rising wage rates, both rural and
urban unemployment have persisted. It is therefore not
possible to apply, except with appropriate and significant
modification, the Lewis model of labor transfer in an underdeveloped country. The combination of an oligopsonistic
labor market which would tend to force wages below their
free market level and Government minimum wage policy
which tends to lift them above the market rate operate to
make the theoretical solution to the wage problem indeterminate. [15]

NON-PECUNIARY PAYMENTS

In addition to money wages and "dash" payments, most
American employers in Liberia provide services or "fringe
benefits" to their employees, the value of which may at times
exceed the basic money wage. Firestone, as the oldest
American business in Liberia and the largest employer, has
developed the most extensive non-wage progress. Other
companies, however, actually have or plan to inaugurate
fringe programs similar to most, if not all, of the Firestone
plans. In fact, it may be said that competition for labor
more frequently takes the form of offering additional fringe
benefits rather than by proferring higher direct money wages.
In addition to the purely utilitarian motive underlying the provision of non-pecuniary benefits to workers, there is also the
recognition of a social obligation by these firms. The president of one of the largest firms said to the writer, shortly
before the latter's departure for Liberia in 1956, " I
hope you recognize that we are meeting our social responsi-
bilities over there. "

Free or Subsidized Food and Supplies

One of the principal fringe benefits is the plan of making
available to the Liberian workers free or subsidized food
and other essential items. Firestone makes a basic rice
ration of eight pounds per week at the price of 3. 5 cents per
pound available to unskilled workers, compared with a retail
price ranging between 7 and 9 cents per pound in recent
years. In addition, a married tapper may purchase an additional four pounds of rice per week at the subsidized price
and everyone is allowed to buy four pounds as a bonus for
having worked six successive days. Should this rice be more
than sufficient for the needs of a worker and his family, he
is allowed to sell the balance at the prevailing retail price.
B. F. Goodrich makes rice available at a subsidized price
of 5 cents per pound, and gives each worker four pounds per
week as a turnout bonus. Firestone maintains a store on
each division which is stocked with a variety of merchandise
for unskilled workers. Most of these items are sold at cost,
but a few are sold at prices below cost. In the latter case,
sales are generally rationed to so many units per month to
each worker. One danger of having only company-owned
stores available is that workers may become involved in a
never-ending cycle of indebtedness to the company. Firestone officials claim that credit buying is discouraged, except
in very special cases. Others claim that some workers are
so in debt that payment would take a long time, thus keeping
them at the plantation much longer than they originally
planned to stay. [16]
The United States Trading Company, a Firestone subsidiary, maintains a large commissary at Harbel, at which a
large variety of imported goods is available. The prices at
USTC are low, the mark-up being 15 per cent over landed
cost. The stated purpose of this low price policy is to cause
other merchants in the plantation area to charge lower
prices. This attempt to foster competition among retailers
has had only a moderate success. Language barriers and
other factors often lead the natives to shop at other places,
although they pay much higher prices. In fact, a native
market exists beside the USTC commissary where products
are bought and sold at prices as much as twice those charged
for identical items at the commissary.

Housing

A second major auxiliary benefit provided by American employers to Liberians is housing. By 1950, Firestone had built more than 10, 000 houses on the plantation for unskilled workers, of the mud wall, thatched roof type.   Classified workers are provided with brick houses having electricity and running water.   By 1955, the Liberia Mining Company had built two hundred houses for unskilled and skilled laborers.   In addition, Liberians in staff and supervisory positions live in single homes similar to those of American and European employees.   Other firms have followed the Firestone pattern but with improvements.   The Western visitor is immediately impressed with the community at Nimba which matches in appearance a modern European housing development.   The major problem encountered by these employers in furnishing housing for their Liberian workers is that of maintaining minimum sanitary conditions and meeting esthetic requirements, while still permitting the residents to maintain their tribal modes of living. Cultural conflicts over the matter of the type and arrangement of houses are claimed to be few, but employers sometimes have had to make modifications of their original housing plans to satisfy their employees.

Education

Educational facilities comprise the third major type or non-monetary emolument offered by foreign employers to their Liberian workers.   Firestone has the most extensive program of education for its employees, but other firms provide facilities which, for the relatively uneducated population of Liberia, provide an essential service.   Fifteen divisional schools staffed by thirty-one teachers are maintained by Firestone.   These schools offer elementary education to children of workers, and literacy education to adults.   Considering that the unskilled labor force at Firestone generally exceeds 20, 000 people, the number of children and workers taking advantage of this free education is small.   In 1955 only about 2, 200 children and 300 adults were regularly registered in these schools on both the Harbel and Maryland County plantations. [17]   Other employers also offer the opportunity

for an elementary education to their workers and families.
However, in most of these cases, the company furnished the
school building and supplies, and the teachers are supplied
by the Liberian Government.

To its classified workers, Firestone offers classroom and
on-the-job vocational education. Advanced students are
granted scholarships to Booker Washington Institute, and in
some cases to foreign educational institutions. Vocational
education programs are in effect at the Liberia Mining Company and LAMCO, the latter being a joint venture between
the Company on the one hand and the Liberian and the Swedish
Governments on the other. At the present time, these company sponsored and operated vocational training programs,
along with Booker Washington Institute, are the only significant efforts of this type in Liberia. Other employers have
not yet reached the stage of development where they have
vocational or scholarship programs for higher education. [18]

Medical Care

The fourth important non-wage benefit is medical and
hospital care. In addition to the fact that the social responsibility of these business firms leads them to provide medical
services, the employers find that such facilities are required
to assure continuous production and operation. Many new
workers suffer from common tropical diseases which prevent them from being efficient workers. These maladies
must be cured before the individual begins work. In addition,
Liberian law holds employers liable for injuries occurring in
the course of employment not attributable to the employee's
negligence or carelessness. Most employers find that the
easiest and surest way of meeting this responsibility is to
provide competent medical care themselves. The Liberia
Mining Company maintains a twenty-five bed, fully equipped
hospital, which could care for seventy-five persons in an
emergency. Firestone operates a one hundred bed hospital on
its main plantation and a smaller hospital at the Cavalla River
plantation. On the larger plantation, nine dispensaries are
located at strategic spots and a dresser is on duty on each
division. The Firestone hospitals jointly cost $500,000 to
build, and the medical budget of this company in recent years
has been in excess of $500,000 per year. [19]

LABOR UNIONS

The Labour Union of Liberia came into existence by Act of the Liberian Legislature in 1949. This union was specifically chartered to cover Liberian employees in the capacity of chauffeurs, mechanics, store boys, washermen, and clerical employees. However, the charter is so written that the union could claim all wage employees, including agricultural workers, as members. The union receives financial support and advice from the Liberian Government. The official United States view, however, is that "there is no indication that the Government is attempting to dominate the organization."[20] Some private commentators disagree with this view, holding that the union is an arm of the True Whig Party, and was fostered to present a facade of democracy to the world.[21]

For many years, the union operated on the fringes of the Liberian labor market. Most Liberian employees of retailing establishments are members, as are Liberians who work as seamen. The majority of the Firestone employees are not members. However, among the classified employees at Firestone, union members can be found. Membership also includes workers at the Port of Monrovia and at the Liberia Mining Company. A few strikes have occurred, mostly over wages and working conditions.[22]

LABOR DISPUTES

The appearance of wage employment on the Liberian economic scene led to innumerable disputes and conflicts between employer and employee. In many instances, the nature of these controversies has been similar to those found in all countries, where some men work for others on a contractual basis. Disputes over wages and other money matters are not uncommon, although Firestone officials report that the incidence of conflicts arising over wage rates is not too frequent. Nevertheless, strikes over wages have occurred at Firestone.[23] The most recent one occurred in 1963 which closed the plantation for a week. Controversies of a special nature regarding money matters must be continuously

coped with by the employer. The fact that so many employees
are illiterate gives rise to misunderstanding about whether
the worker has received the proper amount of pay. When the
employer maintains company stores and the amount of purchases is deducted from the employee's salary, the frequency
of such disputes is increased. Charges of mistreatment are
common. These incidents at times grow out of the cultural
differences between employer and employee and are not
caused by conscious act of the supervisors. [24] Charges are
sometimes brought by workers that European and American
supervisors exhibited racial bias. This type of claim may
sometimes be real, but it may also be a convenient way for a
Liberian to rid himself of a supervisor whom he dislikes
since the penalty of this offense is a $1000 fine and deporta-
tion.

Machinery for settling labor disputes is provided in the
form of labor courts, which are under the administration of
the Department of the Interior. Appeals may be made from
these courts to the appropriate Circuit Court and the Labor
Court decisions may be reviewed by the Supreme Court of
Liberia. Strikes are forbidden prior to the presentation of a
case before the Labor Court, and employers may not fire
strikers, once a legal strike occurs. Some employers maintain their own grievance procedure. If no settlement is
reached privately, disputes so handled must be referred to
the appropriate Labor Court.

LIBERIAN SUPERVISORY PERSONNEL

A potential political danger is found in the policy of those
firms employing non-Liberians in supervisory capacities.
Every concession contains a clause requiring the concessionaire to employ Liberians wherever it is practical. Typical of
such provisions is Article VI of the Concession Agreement
between the Government of the Republic of Liberia and the
B. F. Goodrich Company, dated July 9, 1954.

B. F. Goodrich shall not import unskilled labor for the
carrying out of any operations under the Concession,
including the Accessory Works and Installations, except
in the event that the local labor supply shall prove
inadequate for its needs, and in such event B. F. Goodrich

undertakes to import only such unskilled labor as shall
be acceptable to the Government.

B. F. Goodrich shall endeavor to train Liberian personnel for various positions in said operations. However, all persons deemed by B. F. Goodrich to be
required for the prosecution of its work hereunder,
including executives, officers, engineers, consultants,
technicians, supervisors, planters and any other skilled
or semi-skilled labor shall be granted permission to
enter and reside in the Republic and to depart therefrom;
and the Government undertakes to grant to B. F. Goodrich every assistance in connection therewith to enable
the aforesaid personnel of B. F. Goodrich to carry out
their tasks in the best and most efficient manner.

The Government agrees that it will encourage and assist
the efforts of B. F. Goodrich to secure and maintain an
adequate labor supply, and also will use its offices to
prevent infiltration of radical elements which could
interrupt or affect adversely the operations of B. F.
Goodrich under the Concession or be dangerous to the
peace, tranquility or well-being of the Republic or to
its economic progress.

To date, the Government of Liberia has liberally interpreted the concessionaires' obligation to "endeavor to train
Liberian persons for various positions." No evidence was
discovered by the writer of pressure by the Government upon
the private companies to accelerate and intensify the training
of Liberians for administrative positions. The fact that few
Liberians are employed by these firms in positions higher than
overseer or chief clerk, however, has been severely criticized
by many individual Liberians as well as by some Americans
in Liberia. Foreign concessionaires charge that few Liberians
are sufficiently trained to assume positions of responsibility.
Liberians, and other critics of concession labor policies,
retort that these companies have no executive training program
for Liberians, by which they may rise to managerial positions.
There is, however, some validity in the charge that few
Liberians currently possess administrative skill. Furthermore, few Liberians with such qualifications appear interested

in such employment.   A further explanation of why few
educated Liberians seek employment with large firms is that
trained Liberians frequently find superior opportunities elsewhere, measured in both salary and prestige terms.

Mining companies employ many Liberians in supervisory
and technical positions as do commercial and banking enterprises.   Nevertheless, it is still a fact that when one calls on
the "boss man," he almost invariably confronts a white man.
The cost of maintaining foreign personnel is high, as noted
elsewhere, and reduces taxable profits in addition to being a
source of annoyance, whether justified or not by economic
and technical considerations.

In conclusion, it is desirable to take note of the argument
of H. W. Singer that import-substitution industries are preferred to export industries on the grounds that they generate
external economies through the training of indigenous personnel in management and technical skills.   That export industries have trained Liberians to fill many heretofore unknown
positions with transferable skills certainly cannot be denied.
The question of whether this effect has been maximized by
export industries, however, remains open.   At the same time,
evidence that import-substitution industries provide more
and better linkage effects in the area of manpower training in
Liberia is scarce.   Exports have so far dominated the
economy and import-substitution industries have been almost
absent.   Thus, the question of the relative desirability of one
type of industry versus the other remains an academic one in
the light of Liberian experience.   It can be demonstrated that
some training by export industries has taken place with
resulting external economies redounding to the economy.   But
to assert more than this is conjecture, especially since there
would have been no significant amount of capital formation if
rubber and iron ore had not been exploited by foreign capital.
The domestic market has been and remains too small to
attract most manufacturing industries.   If the Singer argument has validity, it does so when a choice exists between
export and manufacturing industries.   So far, Liberia has not
had the opportunity to make a selection between these alternatives.

FOOTNOTES

1. The special problems of employing skilled and professional personnel are discussed on pages 106-108.

2. This practice was one receiving considerable attention by the League of Nations, which investigated charges of slavery in Liberia in 1931 and 1932. Under pressure from the League and from individual nations, the King administration abolished pawning in the hope of satisfying its critics.

3. Excerpts from a letter from a traveler in the interior to the financial Advisor to Liberia, reprinted in Republic of Liberia, Treasury Department, Annual Report of the Financial Advisor (Monrovia: November 28, 1931), pp. 16-19. Also see Kimble, op. cit., pp. 573-574.

4. The higher bonus during the first six months of the year is paid because this period is the time for preparing farms, making men more difficult to find and to hold.

5. It is assumed by Firestone officials that some people would voluntarily seek jobs to fill requirements. Each paramount chief receives his bonus only if his quota is entirely filled. No bonus payment is made, for example, for 475 men from a chiefdom which had been assigned a quota of 480. However, volunteer workers are counted as part of a chiefdom's quota if their tribe is known by the company.

6. The writer was privileged to accompany Mr. William MacKinnon, General Manager of the Goodrich plantations, on a visit to a village, where he witnessed a vigorous, although friendly, palaver over labor.

7. See page 9 for a discussion of this phenomenon.

8. Taylor, op. cit., p. 69.

9. Idem.

10. Private conversation between Liberia Mining Company officials and the writer.

11. Buell, op. cit., p. 50. Goodrich officials state that

many workers prefer to return to their homes, off the
plantation, each night, despite the fact that they have a
longer walk to and from work each day. In addition, these
workers become liable for hut tax payments which are paid
by the company if the workers live in company housing com-
pounds.

12. Quoted in Anderson, op. cit., p. 136.

13. In 1951, an economic survey of Liberia described the
Kroo Town Corporation, a legal entity, which had pre-
emptory rights to place twenty-five per cent of the Liberians
hired by ships stopping at Liberia. This corporation
received payment from the worker, and frequently the headman of a crew was paid by the worker also. American maritime union hiring halls have not been unique in the use of
this technique. See Litsey, op. cit., p. 32.

14. Permanent disability requires payment of three years'
pay. Lesser injuries are compensated according to a scale
established in the United States Navy Contract NAY9673 for
the construction of the Free Port of Monrovia.

15. The reader is referred to L. G. Reynolds, "Wages and
Employment in a Labor Surplus Economy," American
Economic Review, LV (1965) for a discussion of a similar
divergence between theory and practice in Puerto Rico.

16. The fact that some tappers are in debt to the store causes
trouble at pay time. Most of the unskilled workers are
illiterate and cannot count very well. Considerable palaver
ensues over what is due the worker and what he owes to the
store. Some of these workers, however, do surprisingly
well in counting, through the expedient of collecting a pile of
stones, one for each day worked.

17. Taylor, op. cit., p. 77.

18. Most American business firms in Liberia have also made
contributions to the Liberian educational system. These
contributions of money are made not only to the Liberian
Government but to private mission schools as well.

19.   Firestone, H. S. Jr., "Private Enterprise and Point Four," Vital Speeches, 19 (November 15, 1952), p. 93.

20.   United States Department of Commerce, Establishing A Business in Liberia, (Washington: United States Printing Office, 1954) p. 4.

21.   This is the Party which, almost without interruption, has dominated Liberian politics since 1847.

22.   What was perhaps the first strike in Liberia's history took place in 1945 by the employees of the Raymond Concrete Pile Company, during the construction of the Port of Monrovia.

23.   Taylor, op. cit., p. 88.

24.   Such disputes at times are also encouraged by petty officials. Suits for damages, especially involving alleged defamation of character are an accepted risk, born by foreign employers and supervisors. See Hogue, D., "Liberian Road" Atlantic Monthly, 175 (1945), pp. 61-65; and 175 (1945), pp. 75-78.

5

The utilization of Liberian land and labor resources by foreign private investors has been demonstrated in the preceeding chapters. The next several chapters will examine the contributions of public foreign aid to the development of technical skills and as a supplier of infrastructure capital.

Two extremely important questions directly related to foreign investment will be discussed in this chapter. The first problem relates to the rate of private Liberian investment induced by the inflow of foreign capital. The second issue concerns the financial relationship between foreign investors and the Liberian Government stemming from the fact that the bulk of Government revenue emanates from exports of rubber and iron ore, and that the amount of tax and royalty payments is a function of world prices for these products. This is the classic terms of trade problem of underdeveloped nations and raw material producers noted by Kindleberger and Singer, among others. [1]

PRIVATE LIBERIAN INVESTMENT

The Role of Domestic Private Investment

The merits and necessity of domestic saving and investment, especially from private sources, have been noted by several authorities. Experts of the United Nations and of the International Bank for Reconstruction and Development observe that "the role of foreign finance in economic development can only be of a subordinate character. " [2] Buchanan and Ellis state with great force the case for primary reliance being upon domestic investment. [3]

Unless the habits of consumption and saving, the institutions and legal framework for accumulation, lending and investing can be adapted to the building and maintenance of capital, foreign aid can bring only transitory benefits. A permanent basis for higher living standards must be

created within the society; indeed, this is the very
meaning of economic development. Unless the chief
nurture of growth is indigenous, the society is constantly exposed to retrogression.

This strong preference for private domestic investment is
more than a reflection of the nationalism or xenophobia which
is currently conditioning economic thinking in some underdeveloped areas. It also recognizes the economic fact that,
although foreign financing may serve to "grubstake" the production of social and production capital, a considerable
amount of real capital must be created from domestic
resource supplies.[4] Theoretically, it makes no difference
during the initial state of capital formation whether funds for
development come from foreign or domestic sources since
either source provides the economic surplus necessary for
capital formation. Foreign loans, however, create certain
immediate and long run balance of payments and transfer
problems which are avoided by domestic investment. Furthermore, the supply of foreign capital is less stable than the
supply of domestic capital funds.[5]

There are also compelling political reasons for preferring
domestic to foreign sources of capital funds for economic
development. A particular country's interpretation of international law may be such to cause it to resort to colonial or
imperialist penetration abroad in order to protect the foreign
property of its citizens. Although the flag does not always
follow trade and investment, direct or indirect political
domination by the investor may nevertheless ensue in some
instances.

Supply of Saving

Saving and Income

As in most underdeveloped countries, the majority of the
Liberian people save little or nothing. A broad middle class
of farmers, artisans, and merchants, which saves a significant
portion of the national income in western countries, is not yet
established in Liberia. The few prosperous families there
reputedly invest or hoard large sums abroad or indulge their
desires for expensive homes, furnishings, and for other forms
of conspicuous consumption.[6]

One measure of a nation's capacity to save is its level of
per capita income. [7] For all of tropical Africa, per capita
incomes averaged $50 in 1949 and $100 in 1957. [8] Liberia had
a per capita income averaging less than $100 in 1956 and $127
in 1960. [9]

Table 12: Per Capita Income, Selected African Territories,
           1956-1957.

Territory	Approximate Amount
Ghana (Gold Coast)	$ 194
French West Africa	133
Rhodesia and Nyasaland	132
Malagasy Republic (Madagascar)	119
Liberia	91
Kenya	78
Belgian Congo	76
Sierra Leone	70
Gambia	56-70
Nigeria	69
Uganda	57
Tanganyika	48
Ethiopia	30

Source: United Nations, Economic Survey of Africa Since
1950, (New York: 1959) Reproduced from Kimble, Tropical
Africa, (New York: The Twentieth Century Fund, 1960),
II, 397.

With an average per capita income of this size, no matter
what the cultural factors which frame and determine the
pattern of specific wants, it is not likely that a significant
volume of saving will be forthcoming from the bulk of the
Liberian society. The marginal utility of consumer goods
against that of leisure or capital accumulation is not a matter
of a finely drawn choice between many and varied economic
possibilities. "Wants (in such a society) are to a considerable degree biological and are of the order of survival
itself. " [10] The refined balancing of present against future
goods is not an important element of the economizing process

in a pre-machine economy.

This is merely another way of saying that "people are poor because they are poor" and implies that a rise in income and productivity is necessary to enhance the willingness, as well as the capacity, to save. Once it begins, economic development is a self-propelled process.[11]

Poverty is relative as well as absolute, however. It reflects a "state of mind" resulting from a discrepancy between the level and the standard of living.[12] Duesenberry has postulated an interrelation and interaction of consumer demands which help to explain, for example, why three-quarters of all American families save little or nothing. Poverty, in an absolute sense, is not the cause of this. It results from the desire by people for consumer goods, desires which, for each individual, are enhanced by contact with others who possess them.[13] It is not difficult to understand why, in a society with a per capita income of less than 5 per cent of that in the United States, the propensity to consume is 100 per cent for almost everyone, including those who are "well-off" by that society's standard.

Non-Economic Factors Affecting Saving

Many Liberians, particularly those with higher incomes, are in debt to merchants, banks and individuals. Numerous explanations are offered for this condition, and all probably have some validity. Low incomes are the reason in some cases and a disregard for debt, varying with the level of the individual's position in government, is often cited as another. In other cases, debt is the result of the immutable bonds among relatives. If one person needs money or goods, every member of the clan in the vicinity is expected to contribute to him, often borrowing to meet their obligation.

Whatever the reasons underlying particular cases, Liberians in general have a strong proclivity to spend beyond their incomes. The habit of regular saving is not yet a part of the economic and social pattern. A leading Liberian banker cited several cases of savings accounts, which were started only after much persuasion, but liquidated in a few months for one reason or another and never re-opened. One bank desirous of being "a Liberian Bank for Liberians," permitted only one withdrawal from savings deposits every six months in the first years of its operation.

On the other hand, some examples of saving by even the lowest income people may be found. Collective consumption and production have a counterpart with respect to saving. Among people employed for wages, there is the practice of susu, whereby several people agree that every payday one of them will receive the entire income of the group. While the proceeds of susu are often used for consumption or to meet emergency outlays, they are also used to finance the purchase of a capital asset, such as a truck.

In rural villages, most individual saving, either real or monetary, is applied to the maintenance of certain personages in conspicuous consumption. Little or no net productive capital accumulation results except when a chief may purchase, let us say, a truck for the village or allocate labor to construction of a hut, road, or school building. In the majority of cases, the accumulation of individual wealth is motivated more by the desire for prestige, more sumptuous entertainment or the purchase of another wife, than for more income.

The presence of these unproductive savings clearly indicates that the willingness and in a limited way, the ability to save are present among even the most primitive tribes. The unproductive use of saving most frequently results from a lack of knowledge of how it might be profitably employed. Technical assistance, which brings such knowledge to the villages, may be implemented by a pre-existing supply of savings available for construction of school buildings, clinics, equipment and tools. In order that the people may visualize this potential, however, other shortcomings must also be corrected. Personal property rights must be secured if both saving and its productive use are to be encouraged. Production capital is of little value without social capital such as transportation and marketing facilities to allow the profitable movement and disposal of the product. The state of mind of people afflicted by endemic diseases, ignorance, and poverty is not conducive to a vigorous, healthy, growing economy nor to good management of what natural, human, and capital resources that are available. Profitable local investment, then, depends in large part upon the rate and form of government and foreign investment.

Mobilization of Saving

Role of Banking in an Underdeveloped Economy

The banking system of a country occupies a cardinal position in the complex of forces determining the speed and direction of the nation's economic growth. This is so for two principal reasons. Banks mobilize and direct investment funds into productive investment and serve as a vehicle for the implementation of monetary and credit policies of the government. This latter function is unimportant in Liberia presently as the country has no bank of issue or an independent currency.

While a considerable amount of attention properly has been given to expanding the banking system of Liberia in order to make credit available to interior villages, sufficient emphasis has not been placed upon the equally important function of moving loanable funds from one place to another. The conspicuous consumption found in a typical hinterland town is partly the result of a lack of local investment opportunities, and partly influenced by a lack of institutions designed to transfer saving to investments elsewhere in Liberia. The use of a small accumulated surplus of food or cattle as a dowry or its dissipation for a feast can hardly be justifiably criticized in an economy where there is no mechanism for channeling these surpluses into productive investment of the usual sort. The allocation of investment in an underdeveloped country is as significant as its total magnitude. Because capital is relatively the most scarce factor of production in an underdeveloped economy, the proper employment of what is available becomes a consideration of highest importance. Less than optimum use cannot be tolerated to the same extent as it may in an economy where the magnitude of investment as a determinant of the level of employment is of primary concern. It is a paradox that an economy such as Liberia which must make the most careful allocation of capital, does not possess a capital market through which savings may be allocated to projects having a high private and/or social marginal productivity. While the mere existence of banks is no guarantee that the best allocation will be made of capital funds, it does make available a mechanism which could facilitate the efficient performance of this economic function.

The operations of the seven private banks in Liberia have
been described in Chapter III. It is only necessary to
emphasize here the fact that since these banks do not operate
under the constraint of a Liberian monetary authority, they
conduct their businesses along lines of the commercial loan
principle. Interest rates are 6 per cent or higher for
unsecured loans and 5 per cent for loans secured by commodities, mortgages, or other marketable assets. Commercial credit is generally extended for no more than ninety days
and mortgage loans carry a maturity of from three to five
years. Personal loans are made only to government
employees, secured by a Limited Power of Attorney whereby
the bank may receive interest and principal payments from
the borrower's salary directly from the Treasury Department.

Two Government lending institutions, Agricultural Credit
Corporation and the Liberian Development Corporation,
supplement private banks as a source of funds to private
businesses. Both of these organizations are outgrowths of
the Agricultural and Industrial Credit Corporation which was
activated in 1956.[15] Activities of ACC have thus far been
small. The Corporation has operated with $123,000, which
it assumed from the parent body, plus borrowings from the
Public Law 480 Fund totaling $253,000. The LDC has
received cash contributions from the Liberian budget of
$870,000 with another $185,000 due in 1964. In mid-1964, it
had outstanding loans of $590,000, pending commitments of
$168,000, and contingent liabilities and two guaranteed loans
valued at $110,000 and $473,000 respectively. The LDC also
conducts feasibility studies of potential industrial investment projects, and has promoted some of these opportunities
among private investors. While most of the investment
generated by the LDC has been from foreign sources, it has
managed to stimulate some Liberian participation in these
projects.

The Liberian Development Bank was activated in 1963, but
by 1964 had not made any loans or investments. The Bank
has an authorized capital of $10 million of which $3 million
has already been supplied from a portion of the proceeds of a
multipurpose loan from the Federal Republic of Germany to
the Liberian Government, with which the Government has
purchased some of the Bank's stock. Private Liberians have

also made some contribution to the capital of the Liberian
Development Bank.[16]

While the amount of funds available to finance domestic
private investment is not enormous, it does not appear
that a scarcity of capital funds nor of institutions to mobilize
domestic and foreign savings is exerting the principal
restraint on Liberian business expansion. What is lacking
according to both bankers and development planners is a
shortage of bankable projects. Cited as a major reason for
the paucity of viable Liberian private investment projects is
the scarcity of entrepreneurs.

Liberian Business Enterprises

Almost all facets of Liberian economic activity are dominated by foreign investors. Even in commercial agriculture,
the largest firms are foreign-owned and serve as the principal source of revenue and employment, despite the more
than 2,000 Liberian rubber producers. Private Liberian
investment is most in evidence in the service trades; but in
almost every line of business, foreign operations are dominant. On Monrovia's Waterside, the commercial center of the
country, no more than two or three Liberian stores may be
found in a total of thirty-five or more. In Kakata, the main
street is lined with stores, but only one is Liberian-owned.
Many small Liberian-owned stores are found in towns and
along highways, their main stock in trade being cigarets,
beer and a few food staples. The large hotels and restaurants
are foreign-owned; Liberian owned and operated hotels and
restaurants are small. On the other hand, Liberian entrepreneurship is dominant in tailoring and dry cleaning, barbering,
taxi companies, and motor truck transportation.

In the professional fields, the number of Liberians is
steadily increasing. Although more than one-half of the
doctors are foreigners, the number of Liberian doctors is
considerably greater than it was a decade ago. Only in the
legal profession are no foreigners found, as only Liberian
citizens may be admitted to the bar. Six of the seven banks
operating in 1964 were wholly foreign-owned and the remaining one has large foreign stockholders.

The number of Liberian tradesmen and artisans is increasing every year, and a small but significant number of

craftsmen are going into business for themselves. Nevertheless, foreign firms or the Liberian Government are the
principal employers of such persons. A cinder block plant,
two or three construction enterprises, a shoe factory, and
a paint company are the only Liberian manufacturing enterprises of any size.

One final fact regarding investment by Liberians in
Liberia must be noted. The wealthy families have preferred
in the past to invest in either urban or agricultural real
estate, or place their funds abroad. There is no way of
ascertaining the total volume of private Liberian expatriated
wealth, but it is widely opined that the amount is considerable. Foreign investment by Liberians is not entirely fruit-
less, as hoarding of money would be, for some contribution
is made to the national income, in the form of interest and
profit receipts. It is doubtful, however, that this contribution equals that which would be realized if this wealth were
invested in domestic ventures.

Why Don't More Liberians Enter Private Business ?

If the profit motive is accepted as the basic cause of
private investment, then the most significant proximate
cause of private investment is the nature and size of the
market for the product. The size of the market, according
to Nurske, is affected only slightly by the size of the population or volume of physical resources available. The primary
determinant of the size of the market is the kind and amount
of capital which people use. [17] Because of the dependency
upon the size of the market, a strong interrelation exists
between individual investment projects. The argument is
that one firm cannot expand faster than the entire economy.
The aggregate level of income in turn is determined in part
by the rate and kind of investment going on in a country. To
the extent that the marginal productivity of capital in a particular use depends upon the level of national income, one
firm will not find it profitable to expand at a faster rate than
that of the pack. Balanced growth then, becomes as important a determinant of economic progress as the over-all rate
of growth. However, this circular dependency of investment and income may cause economic stagnation and a per-
petuation of a low-level income equilibrium. If little or no

investment takes place, a static market is created.

A counter-argument to the Nurske "balanced growth" thesis is offered by Hirschman.[18] In this model, tensions and disequilibuium are the prime movers of the development process. The machinery by which development proceeds is through the linkage connecting each particular economic process with all others. The nature of development is conceptualized by an input-output matrix; the basic development planning problem being to select the cells having the strongest linkage effects. These are the sectors which should be expanded first in order to create a disequilibrium in directly linked factor or commodity markets. The response of these markets to the purposefully generated disequilibrium, or tension, propels the economy along its growth path. The development strategy should be to select the sequence of projects which maximizes the induced investment, rather than to chose a package of current projects which maximizes discounted marginal social product. Hirschman suggests that the oft followed policy of giving priority to social overhead capital on the assumption that an excess supply of roads or electricity will generate private investment is a policy which is too permissive and which has too uncertain an outcome. A modest shortage of such facilities will not handicap productive capital investment. In fact, the result may be a more rapid rate of total investment as social capital is formed to meet the excess demand than that realized by the reverse.[19]

Both the Nurske and Hirschman theses fail to answer fully the question under consideration here; namely, why are Liberians reluctant to enter business on a large scale, except for rubber production?[20] The principal investments in Liberia have been in export industries, not in production for domestic sale in response to internal market conditions. To the extent that the large firms have created a demand for Liberian goods or services, it has been foreign investors generally which have filled demand. In fact, the inflow of foreign capital has created a Hirschman-type disequilibrium in which the demand for social overhead services, such as roads and power, or for privately produced products and services, such as food and supplies, has exceeded the supply. The shortage of social overhead capital projects has become so acute that present development plans center upon these. However, the private sector has not yet responded in a vigorous way to this demand.

A wide variety of reasons, some real and some con-
jectural, have been advanced to explain the lack of response
of Liberian enterprise to a rising demand. This multitude
of causes reduces to three general types: lack of capital;
social attitudes which mitigate against individual enterprise;
and a lack of technical and managerial skills. Arranged
according to these groupings, the most frequently stated
causes of a deficiency of private Liberian investment may be
summarized as follows:[21]

I. Lack of capital resources.
  A. An unwillingness to invest jointly, either with other
      Liberians or with foreigners. The operation in
      the past of a number of promoters who turned out
      to be "con" men is allegedly an important con-
      tributing factor to the attitude of suspicion.

  B. Inadequate banking facilities.
      1. The banks are unsympathetic to the needs of
          Liberian businessmen.
      2. The banks have not sought out opportunities to
          assist borrowers.
      3. The attitude of bankers is too conservative, as
          shown by the terms of lending. Most loans are
          for less than six months and interest rates are
          6 per cent or higher.
      4. The banks do not always understand the partic-
          ular credit needs of the individual borrower and
          do not "tailor make" credit to fit the borrower's
          requirements, as American banks are learning
          to do.

  C. The largest savers are foreign businesses which
      transfer profits abroad, rendering them unavailable
      for domestic use by others, or investing them
      directly in their own enterprises. Transfer of
      earnings in 1960 by concessions amounted to 27 per
      cent of Gross Domestic Money Income.

  D. Lack of personal saving.
      1. Conspicuous consumption and high propensity to
          import consumer goods by the higher income

groups have dissipated personal saving.

2. Most people do not have the thrift habit.

3. Saving of wealthy Liberians has been invested abroad, rather than locally.

4. The basic cause of saving by most people is low income. This is particularly true in Monrovia where most activity is with money and where inflation has worked to reduce real incomes.

5. The only banks which can mobilize money savings for lending are in Monrovia or coastal towns, hence a great amount of potential investment funds are lost to the economy.

E. Capital formation occurs in villages, by producing more than is currently consumed, but this does not involve money capital for the most part. Even where village activity leads to the sale of cash crops, savings are not available to other groups because of the lack of banking facilities and because of tribal customs of self-sufficiency.

II. Social attitudes

A. Until recently, those who could invest exhibited a disdainful attitude toward manual work, which many forms of business would require.

B. An attitude of pragmatism leads to trying something new only after it is proven worthwhile. This inhibition checks internal investment as no one is willing to be the first to innovate.

C. Prestige of government work drains competent man-power from the private sector.

III. Lack of knowledge

A. The early settlers had many skills which were allowed to die out. The tribal peoples have only recently been exposed to a way of life and an education system teaching such skills as auto mechanics or carpentry.

B.   The higher level of technical knowledge necessary
     for the organization and administration of large
     businesses has been lacking.

The new elite is causing some of the deterrents to
become weaker, such as personal attitudes toward private
investment. In other cases, however, a more direct attack
through government sponsorship of new businesses, indirect
assistance such as a judicious use of protective tariffs, or
preferential buying from Liberian firms may be warranted.

TERMS OF TRADE AND ECONOMIC DEVELOPMENT

Dependence on Exports

The role of exports in the Liberian economy--particularly
of those produced by foreign investors--may be demonstrated
by a syllogism. The major premise is that saving is
necessary to finance developmental projects, an assumption
which will not be questioned. The minor premise holds that
the Government is the only source of saving of any consequence. This premise requires some elaboration.

It has been noted previously that the amount of private
Liberian saving is small. What little there has been in the
past was either invested in real estate speculation or exported.
In 1960, private saving was estimated at $1.2 million plus or
minus $3 million. [22] Even if the suggested margin of error
is positive, the annual rate of saving is not a promising pros-
pect for financing major development projects in the near
future. The Bureau of Economic Research and Statistics
suggests that this saving could not be tapped by the Government except at an interest rate which compared favorably
with the returns to private investment, and which would most
likely have to exceed 15 per cent per annum. [23]

The major portion of Liberian economic development must
be financed either by foreign private capital or by the Government itself. Government borrowing has been utilized extensively in recent years to expedite construction of capital
projects. But the ability to borrow and the terms of loans
which have been granted have been predicated upon the state
of the budget. Revenues have exhibited a steady advance

since 1940, as shown in Table 13. In that year, less than $1
million was collected, almost all of which was from customs
revenue. By 1950, the budget reached $4 million, followed
by an unusually sharp increase in 1951 due to the payment by
Firestone of income taxes of $7 million. In 1953, iron ore
royalties amounting to $2 million were received for the first
time and other new taxes such as sales tax, luxury tax, and
per capita health tax began to yield significant returns. In
addition, shipping registration fees achieved a prominent
position in the Liberian fiscal system. Revenues increased
by 300 per cent between 1940 and 1950, and 350 per cent
between 1950 and 1955. During the latter period (1950-1955),
Gross Domestic Income approximately doubled. It is evident
that the Government was making a major encroachment upon
both the private Liberian and foreign sectors.

However, this rate of expansion has not continued. Between
1956 and 1960, revenues rose by 81 per cent, and if revenue
estimates for 1965 of $41 million are firm, the increase in the
quinquennium from 1961 to 1965 will be only 21 per cent. The
rate of revenue growth is expected to accelerate slightly
after 1965, however, with estimated revenues in 1968 of $50
million producing a 25 per cent rise over 1965.

From the budget comes the funds for public capital formation and developmental projects. Beginning in 1952, the
Government allocated 20 per cent of the budget of the Joint
Commission under the terms of the agreement with the
United States in 1951. This requirement has been firmly met
ever since, although it has become increasingly difficult to
determine the exact uses of this appropriation. With the
Joint Commission scheduled to expire in 1965, it is uncertain
whether this requirement by the United States will continue
in force. However, the development needs of the country
continue to grow while, at the same time, past projects exert
a rising claim on the budget for operating funds.

The last third of the syllogism now becomes clear. The
profits of concessions hold the key to the future ability of the
Liberian Government to finance economic development. One
index of the source of such funds is exports. Table 13
indicates that the export trend has been decidedly upward
but with some erratic, and at times even violent, fluctuations.
Part of the explanation of these movements is found in
changes in production volume. But the principal cause of

fluctuations has been instability of export prices, especially
of rubber and iron ore.

Table 13: Budget Receipts, Exports, Imports, and Trade
           Balance--Liberia, 1940-62 (millions of dollars)

Year	Budget Receipts	Exports	Imports	Trade Balance
1940	0. 9	3. 3	2. 2	1. 1
1941	1. 2	5. 0	3. 3	1. 7
1942	1. 0	6. 8	3. 9	2. 9
1943	1. 3	9. 0	4. 0	5. 0
1944	1. 6	10. 3	3. 0	7. 3
1945	1. 9	11. 3	3. 5	7. 8
1946	2. 3	12. 3	4. 7	7. 6
1947	3. 2	13. 1	8. 8	4. 3
1948	3. 4	15. 8	8. 8	7. 0
1949	3. 8	15. 5	8. 2	7. 3
1950	3. 9	27. 6	10. 6	17. 1
1951	12. 8	52. 1	17. 1	35. 0
1952	8. 9	37. 2	18. 2	19. 0
1953	10. 6	31. 0	18. 7	12. 3
1954	11. 9	26. 4	22. 7	3. 7
1955	15. 3	42. 9	26. 0	16. 9
1956	17. 9	44. 5	26. 8	17. 7
1957	20. 0	40. 4	38. 3	2. 1
1958	18. 1	53. 8	38. 5	15. 3
1959	24. 6	66. 9	42. 9	24. 0
1960	32. 4	82. 6	69. 2	13. 4
1961	33. 0	61. 9	90. 7	-28. 8
1962	37. 0	67. 5	132. 2	-64. 7

Source: Steadman, Report on the Fiscal System of Liberia,
Republic of Liberia, Bureau of Statistics, Foreign Trade
Supplement, 1956, (Monrovia: 1956).

RUBBER PRICES AND INCOMES

Price Movements

The price of natural rubber is established in a world market within which Liberian production amounts to only 2 per cent of the total. Liberian producers accept the price as a datum, and respond to it with increased tapping in the short run and additional planting in the long run. The only aspect of adjustment to a changed market over which Liberian producers have control is the level of costs.

Rubber prices have been subjected to both short-term fluctuations and a long-term decline, a development common to most agricultural products. From Table 14 it is apparent that high prices coincide with periods of high demand in industrial countries and low prices with periods of industrial recession. The effect of World War II is seen in the rise in unit value of 57 per cent between 1940 and 1944, although the reported increase does not fully reflect the demand-supply imbalance of those years because of price control in the United States. The sharp drop in 1949 was caused by the recession in the United States in 1948-1949. Conversely, the impact of the Korean War is evident in the almost tripling of prices between 1950 and 1951. In 1953 prices fell by 50 per cent compared to 1952.

The impact of two wars and a recession in the United States partially affected a long-run decline in rubber prices which is still occurring. Nevertheless, the deterioration is being strongly felt by rubber producers, and they expect no long-run recovery. Two main factors determine the long-run trend of rubber prices. The first is the chemical property of the substance which controls the rate of technical substitution between natural and synthetic rubber. Firestone officials state that the chemical nature of rubber presently guarantees to it about 20 per cent of the total market at current prices. The second factor, and currently the more important one, is the competition offered to natural rubber by synthetic rubber. Production of synthetic rubber has

increased by more than 150 per cent between 1952 and 1962
while the output of natural rubber over the same period rose
by only 17. 6 per cent.   More significantly, synthetic output
exceeded natural production for the first time in 1962.   Consumption in that year was about the same for each, with
natural rubber holding a precarious edge.   Synthetic production is bound to continue to expand, and this product may
claim as much as 60 per cent of the total rubber market by
1966.   Consequently, the prevailing price of synthetic rubber
has become a major parameter in the demand for natural
rubber.   Coupled with the absolute and relative ascendency of
synthetic production is the fact that this industry is capable
of reducing costs with increased volume.   To the extent that
competition acts to lower synthetic prices accordingly,   the
price of natural rubber will continue to decline.

Table 14:   Rubber Exports by Volume and Value--Liberia,
1940-55 and 1959-62

Year*	Volume (thousands of long tons)	Value (millions of dollars)	Value per ton
1940	6. 3	2. 2	352
1941	8. 1	3. 6	441
1942	11. 6	6. 1	529
1943	13. 1	8. 1	615
1944	17. 1	9. 4	551
1945	19. 8	11. 0	563
1946	20. 1	11. 5	570
1947	24. 8	11. 8	475
1948	17. 4	12. 0	690
1949	28. 5	11. 1	388
1950	34. 2	15. 0	438
1951	37. 2	45. 0	1, 300
1952	24. 4	31. 6	1, 258
1953	34. 2	21. 1	616
1954	34. 1	18. 7	549
1955	38. 7	33. 0	855
1959	44. 5	30. 7	689
1960	48. 5	39. 1	805

Table 14 cont.

Year*	Volume	Value	Value per ton
1961	41. 3	25. 5	617
1962	45. 5	25. 7	563

*Fiscal years 1940-52 (September-August), Calendar years 1953-55 and 1959-62.

Source: Litsey, Annual Economic Review, 1952 . Foreign Operations Administration, United States Operations Mission Dispatch FA-112 , (Monrovia: January 8, 1954). Republic of Liberia, Treasury Department, Bureau of Revenue, Statistical Summaries of Imports, Exports and Shipping for the Year Ending August 31, 1950, (Monrovia: 1951). Republic of Liberia, Bureau of Statistics, Foreign Trade Supplement (Monrovia: 1956). Republic of Liberia, Office of National Planning, Annual Report, 1962-63, (Monrovia: 1963).

With 60 per cent of the market firmly committed to synthetic rubber and 20 per cent reserved for natural, the remaining share is open to whichever producer is able to supply the product at the lowest price. Unfortunately, natural rubber is chemically stable and is not able to be altered. Synthetic rubber, on the other hand, is constantly being technically changed and improved to meet specific demands. It is this capability of synthetic rubber to be designed for a specific use which cost the natural industry the loss of two-thirds of the United States automobile tire market by 1962. [24]

This combination of economic and technical forces does not indicate much likelihood of a reversal of the downward price trend of natural rubber in the forseeable future. The industry may be able to successfully market its future output if economic expansion in user countries is sufficient to overcome the technical advances and price declines of synthetic rubber. But a recapture of lost markets and a rise in the relative share of the total market seem very unlikely.

Rubber Production Costs

Liberian rubber producers, in addition to having to cope with externally determined price movements, must adjust to internal cost changes. The most important cost element in recent years has been wages, including fringe benefits, the trend of which has been upward for the entire economy. Direct labor cost for the Firestone plantation is eight cents per pound of dry rubber. Under the impetus of the last minimum wage increase, the average cost per tapper per day rose to $1.20, which includes an imputed value for non-money benefits. For other large plantations the direct labor cost is approximately equal to that of Firestone. A yield of sixteen pounds of DRC rubber per tapper returns to these producers a margin which is adequate to cover fixed costs and produce net profits. The average daily yield per task for all Liberian producers is reported to be five pounds. Most of this rubber was sold to Firestone at a price between 15.8 and 17.8 cents per pound in 1964. At this price, the average value of output per tapper per day is between eighty and ninety cents. With the minimum wage at sixty-four cents per day, little remains for the average farms to cover other costs. Farms experiencing below average productivity operate at a loss.

The reasons for rising wage rates have been explored in Chapter 4. At the same time that wage costs are increasing physical productivity at Firestone is exhibiting a downward movement because old trees which have passed their peak yielding age constitute a large percentage of the total plantation. The largest independent producers have yields equal to or slightly in excess of that at Firestone because they have the advantage of a larger percentage of higher yielding trees than does Firestone. For the majority of Liberian producers, however, productivity per tapper (and per acre) is low because (1) many of the farms are small, (2) most managers and workers are ignorant of even simple techniques to increase output and/or (3), the farms are operated under conditions of absentee ownership. Of these three causes of low productivity, the last mentioned is considered by many competent authorities to be the most important.

The large producers are attempting to meet the threat of the rising labor cost-declining price squeeze by increasing

tapper productivity. A more capital-intensive process is
being introduced through replacment of older species by
higher yielding trees. Attempts to reduce labor input by an
increase of the task size per tapper have not been successful due to strong labor resistance. Liberian tappers traditionally have a task of 300 trees in contrast to 450 trees for
a Malaysian rubber tapper. Liberian plantation operators
admit, however, that even if a task of 450 trees could be
established, there would remain the problem of transporting
the larger quantity of rubber from the tapping site to collection points.

Table 15: World Production and Consumption of Natural
           and Synthetic Rubber, 1952-1962 (Thousands of
           Metric Tons)

Year	Natural Rubber		Synthetic Rubber	
	Production	Consumption	Production	Consumption
1952	1,790	1,468	878	885
1953	1,728	1,655	936	873
1954	1,810	1,780	716	740
1955	1,918	1,890	1,085	1,065
1956	1,888	1,875	1,211	1,135
1957	1,903	1,898	1,263	1,260
1958	1,940	2,010	1,244	1,255
1959	2,040	2,118	1,635	1,580
1960	1,980	2,065	1,883	1,798
1961	2,090	2,135	1,975	1,920
1962	2,105	2,188	2,240	2,170

Source: Rubber Statistical Bulletin, August, 1963, pp. 2, 9, 21,
27.

For the average rubber farmer, a considerable increase
in productivity is possible without having to resort to the
expensive replacing of trees or breaking with tradition on
task size. Improved tapping and tree care techniques and
more careful processing of rubber could greatly increase the
value of output. In addition, close and constant supervision
of the farm by the owner could convert a loss on farms of

more than twenty-five acres into a profit.

For many rubber producers in Liberia, there is little hope that the financial picture will improve in the immediate future. If productivity on these farms can be increased, losses may be converted into profits--and hence into government revenues or private saving. The long-run prize of higher income will go only to those farms which continue to adopt the latest techniques and which operate at maximum efficiency.

IRON ORE PRICES AND INCOMES

Iron ore prices rose steadily until 1960, in which year Liberia received a gross income per ton of $11.90 (see Table 16). Prices have declined since, reaching an average per ton value of $7.03 in 1963. Offsetting the price fall was an expansion of output over this period which led to the total value of ore exported rising by 60 per cent between 1959 and 1963.

The impact of this diversity in the movement of prices and output most directly reflects itself in Government revenues. In 1962, iron ore royalties amount to 5.1 million compared to $5.7 million in 1961. This decline in revenue in the face of a 32 per cent increase in volume is explained by a 17 per cent fall in price. As other mines enter production, royalty payments will exhibit an absolute rise. When the four existing mines reach their aggregate capacity output level of 17 million tons, the Liberian Government should realize an annual income from this source of about $22 million. If the 1960-61 price level could be re-established, Government income from mining would amount to about $29-$30 million annually. While world iron ore demand is rising, the development of ore deposits is expanding at an even faster rate so that there is little likelihood of a return to these prices. [25]

THE DEVELOPMENT GAP

The decline both of the prices of principal export commodities and of taxable profits of the producers has created a serious budget crisis in Liberia. The nature of the crisis

Table 16: Iron Ore Exports by Volume and Value--
Liberia, 1959-63

| Year | Quantity | | Value | | |
	tons (a)	per cent (b)	dollars (c)	per cent (d)	unit price
1959	2. 6	--	28. 2	--	9. 20
1960	2. 9	11. 6	34. 6	23. 8	11. 90
1961	2. 8	- 3. 4	29. 4	- 15. 1	10. 50
1962	3. 7	32. 2	32. 4	10. 2	8. 66
1963	6. 4	73. 3	45. 0	39. 0	7. 03

(a) millions of long tons
(b) percentage change over previous year
(c) millions of U. S. dollars
(d) percentage change over previous year

Source: Office of National Planning, Annual Report, 1963-64,
(Monrovia: 1964).

is the excess of fixed expenditures plus the cost of development projects over total revenue. This difference is
termed the "development gap, " which is calculated by adding
to the regular budget in a base year the debt retirement
commitments, planned development expenditures, and the
added operating costs arising from the completion of development projects, and subtracting from this total estimated
revenues for each year.

In 1964, planned capital projects of the Government totaled
$92 million of which $15. 9 million had already been spent (see
Table 17). Of the remainder, $57 million was covered by
foreign credits. This left some $19 million, for the period
1965-69, to be provided from current revenues. Except for
the Mount Coffee Hydro project which is to be self-liquidating,
the completion of these projects will cause the regular operating budget to increase by $3. 4 million in 1968 over that of
1964.

On the basis of revenue forecasts made in 1964, a deficit is
predicted of more than $7 million both in 1965 and 1966. In
1967, a balance will be attained, and a substantial surplus

will appear in 1969. This outcome is predicated upon the
completion on schedule of high priority projects, as of 1964;
but with no additional development projects being undertaken.
However, in 1964, a group of projects having slightly lower
priority than those noted above and totaling $41 million were
under consideration by the planning authorities. Unless the
capital, and in some cases the operating cost, of these
secondary projects can be externally financed, it is expected
that only a few of them will be implemented during the next
five years.

The foregoing estimates of the development gap represent
the most optimistic projection of the state of the budget. If
the budget were related to "needs"--defined as projects being
urgently required and having a high pay-off--rather than to
present plans, the development deficit would be several millions of dollars larger for each of the next five years.
Revenues for 1968 are predicted to be $50 million, predicated
on iron ore prices at 1962 levels. At 1961 prices, this total
would rise to at least $57 million. The extent of this loss is
dramatically demonstrated by observing that the predicted
deficit of $7 million for both 1965 and 1966 is twice the present
education budget, or equal to the cost of the para-medical
center presently under construction, or sufficient to finance
the construction of either twenty elementary schools in Monrovia or 350 rural school buildings.

Table 17: Planned Public Capital Projects by Sector--
          Liberia 1964-68 (Thousands of Dollars)

Sector	First Priority Total Cost	Second Priority Total Cost
Education	5,689	6,327
Agriculture	969	4,000
Public Health	6,924	1,550
Highways	36,216	14,021
Univ. of Liberia	1,416	--
Interior	--	300

Table 17 continued

Sector	First Priority Total Cost	Second Priority Total Cost
Post Office	4,968	--
Commerce (airfields)	--	6,093
Liberian Information Service	40	--
Monrovia Sanitation	133	--
Defense	436	--
Public Utility Authority	35,000	9,000
TOTAL	91,791	41,291

Source: Office of National Planning, Annual Report 1964-65.
(Monrovia: 1965).

Table 18:   Estimate of the Development Gap--Liberia,
            1965-68   (Millions of Dollars)

Year	Non-Development Budget Base*	GOL Capital Costs for Projects	Cumulative Increase in GOL Operating Costs	Revenue Estimate **	Surplus or Deficit
1965	39.9	7.3	1.1	41.0	- 7.3
1966	40.5	7.7	2.0	43.0	- 7.2
1967	40.9	1.7	2.7	46.0	0.7
1968	40.9	1.0	3.0	50.0	5.1*

* 1964 Non-Development Budget of $29.6 million, plus projected
  debt service.
**Based on data in Final Report of Klein & Saks Technical
Advisory Mission to National Planning Agency of the Government of Liberia, Klein & Saks, Inc., Wash., D.C., Aug.1964, p. 28.

FOOTNOTES

1. C. P. Kindleberger, "The Terms of Trade and Economic Development", The Review of Economics and Statistics, XL Supplement (1958), pp. 72-85.

2. United Nations, Department of Economic Affairs, Methods of Financing Economic Development in Underdeveloped Areas, (Lake Success, New York: 1949), p. 94. See also International Bank for Reconstruction and Development, The Economic Development of Nigeria, (Baltimore: John Hopkins Press, 1955), pp. 20-21.

3. Buchanan and Ellis, op. cit., p. 301.

4. N. S. Buchanan, International Investment and Domestic Welfare, (New York: Henry Holt, 1945), Chapter I.

5. External influences compound the number of factors determining the supply of foreign funds to a country. For example, domestic activity in the United States Stock Market in 1928-29 caused a diminution in foreign lending by the United States after June, 1928. Net long term capital exports by the United States declined from $847 million in 1928 to $278 million in 1929, a 67 per cent decline. H. B. Lary, The United in the World Economy, (Washington: United States Government Printing Office, 1943), pp. 98-99 and Table I, p. 216.

6. A feature characteristic of other underdeveloped areas. During the period from June 1950 to June 1951, automobile imports into Latin America and Near East countries increased by more than 100 per cent. United Nations, Department of Economic Affairs, World Economic Report 1950-51, (New York: 1952), p. 100. The Liberian balance of payments for 1954 estimates private capital outflow of $4.6 million. This entire amount is shown as an increase in bank balances abroad. Only a minute fraction of the Liberian population is responsible for this capital outflow. This sum, if invested locally instead of abroad, would make a significant contribution to Liberia's economic development.

7. The correlation between levels of income and rate of

domestic capital formation is very loose. See C. P. Kindleberger, Economic Development, 2nd ed. (New York: McGraw-
Hill, 1964), pp. 98-99. The connection between household
incomes and domestic saving is closer, however. The major
reason is that in early stages of development, a large share
of domestic capital formation is sponsored by governments
which finance development projects from foreign loans or
income derived from foreign concessions. Household savings
become an increasing source of domestic capital formation
as income grows.

8. United Nations, Review of Economic Conditions in Africa,
(New York: 1951), p. 6.

9. Derived from a Gross Domestic Money Income of $172.9
million less concession profits and reserves after taxes of
$45.7 million.

10. M. J. Herskovits, Economic Anthropology, (New York:
Alfred A. Knopf, 1952), p. 10.

11. Devoting a share of a rising income to capital formation
is a milder requirement than absolute decrease in consumption. Yet this is extraordinarily difficult to obtain.
Buchanan and Ellis, op. cit., p. 303. Writers have stressed
the cumulative effects of saving which make an absolute
incursion upon living standards unnecessary. See Adler,
"The Fiscal and Monetary Implementation of Development
Programs", American Economic Review, XLII, (1952), 597-
598.

12. Level of Living here denotes the realized or attained real
income position. Standard of Living refers to that income
desired or aimed for by a society. See M. K. Bennett, "International Disparities in Consumption Levels, " American
Economic Review, XLI (1951), 632.

13. J. S. Duesenberry, Income, Saving and the Theory of
Consumer Behavior, (Cambridge: Harvard University Press,
1949), pp. 27, 39. Nurkse terms this propensity to imitate
the consumption of others the "demonstration effect." See
R. Nurkse, "Some International Aspects of the Problem of

Economic Development, " American Economic Review, XLII
(1952), 571-583.

14. "A very poor society might find it extremely hard to do
any saving even if it knew nothing about higher living standards
in the outside world. The vicious circle that tends to keep
down the volume of saving in low-income countries is bad
enough by itself. The point is that it is made even worse by
the stresses that arise from relative as distinct from absolute poverty. " Nurkse, op. cit. , p. 579.

15. Liberian Age, August 27, 1956, p. 1, ff. See Republic
of Liberia, Department of State, "An Act to Create an Agricultural and Industrial Credit Corporation, " Acts Passed by
the Legislature of the Republic of Liberia During the Session
1952-1953, (Monrovia: Government Printing Office, 1953),
pp. 18-21.

16. Liberia is also a member of the African Development
Bank, which operates under the Economic Commission for
Africa. The initial Liberian subscription of $250, 000 was
paid in 1964.

17. Nurkse, Problems of Capital Formation in Underdeveloped
Countries , pp. 18-19.

18. A. O. Hirschman, The Strategy of Economic Development,
(New Haven: Yale University Press, 1958).

19. Ibid. , pp. 94-95.

20. In the case of rubber investment, Firestone may be
regarded as playing the role of a social overhead capital
investor, inasmuch as this company generates external economies accruing to the benefit of smaller producers.

21. It is very important to treat these causes as allegations,
not as facts, and note that individuals do not offer all of these
reasons. For a discussion of barriers to private investment
in Nigeria which are also applicable to Liberia, see C. H.
Olmstead, "Private Investment in Nigeria, " in W. H.
Hausman, Managing Economic Development in Africa,

(Cambridge: The MIT Press, 1963), pp. 90-99.

22. Bureau of Economic Research and Statistics, Annual
Report 1960-1961, p. 43.

23. Loc. cit.

24. Rubber Statistical Bulletin, August 1963, p. 36. The
reader is also referred to the following: New York Times,
September 1, 1963; Barrons' August 19, 1963; London Daily
Telegraph, September 17, 1963.

25. See Office of National Planning, Annual Report, 1962-63,
for an analysis of the world iron ore market vis-a-vis
Liberia.

26. Office of National Planning, Annual Report, 1963-1964.

CHAPTER **6** EXTERNAL AID
TO LIBERIA

UNITED STATES INTERESTS IN LIBERIA

The United States historically has been the principal source
of foreign economic assistance to Liberia, and the U. S.
continues to hold this paramount position despite the absolute
expansion of the flow of aid from other governments and from
the United Nations. It appears that other aid donors have
informally agreed that there exists a special relationship
between Liberia and the United States which bestows on the
United States the primary responsibility for financing and
guiding Liberia's economic development.

Although United States foreign aid policy and strategy have
undergone innumerable shifts since 1940, Liberia has
remained a consistent, albeit small, recipient of aid funds
through almost the entire period during which foreign aid has
been an integral part of the United States budget. A "special
relationship" between the two governments based upon the
role of the United States in Liberia's founding and early years
is not to be discounted as a motivation for United States concern about Liberia's economic welfare. However, during the
first ninety-four years of Liberia's history, the "special
relationship" failed to generate a particularly active participation by the United States in Liberia's economic development.
United States foreign economic assistance has also been
explained as a manifestation of the humanitarian spirit of that
country. But this motivation did not overtly appear until
after 1951. [1]

The actual appearance of an United States economic aid
mission in Liberia was a direct outgrowth of the selection of
Liberia by military strategists to serve as a site for an airfield during World War II. Accompanying the United States
troops stationed in Liberia were public health officers, whose
initial concern was with sanitation conditions for the military
personnel. But efforts to combat malaria, parasites and
other public health hazards inevitably were expanded to
include treatment of afflicted Liberians, and finally to the

establishment of an informal liaison between the United States
Army and the Liberian National Public Health Service. Also
involved in the military considerations underlying assistance
to Liberia was the desire in 1942 for a naval base in West
Africa. Although the military conditions which prompted this
desire subsided after 1944, the decision to build a port was
implemented nevertheless.

United States aid to Liberia also may be partly explained
as being an instrument designed to promote United States
private investment abroad. The post-war reasons for building the Port of Monrovia and the Export-Import Bank Loan
to the Liberia Mining Company in 1948 must be viewed as
examples of this motivation. In 1946, Liberia was the only
independent nation on the West African coast and one of the
three independent nations in all of Sub-Sahara Africa. If
the United States were to establish a commercial and economic
foothold on this continent, the most logical approach would be
through one or more of these countries. The fact that the two
oldest United States foreign aid missions in Africa are in
Liberia and Ethopia lends credence to this motivation for
foreign aid.

Finally, during World War II, Liberia was the only supplier
of natural rubber of any consequence following the Japanese
conquest of Southeast Asia. Because of the severe drain by
war production on the domestic United States supply of iron
ore, Liberia assumed a strategic position because of her
supply of this basic commodity. While Liberian production
of neither of these commodities is as vital today as it was in
the nineteen forties, the protection and development of these
resources played an important role in United States aid
strategy decisions during those years.

More recently, United States interest in Liberia's
economic development has taken on a new dimension because
of the rapid and unpredictable rate of political change in
Africa. With communist control being a serious threat in
several of the newly independent African nations and a reality
in one of them, the success of the Liberian model of development is vital to United States and western prestige. Being
identified with the colonial powers has at times been something of a handicap for the United States in Africa. While
this "stigma" has been less of a problem in Liberia than elsewhere, it is considered mandatory that aid be extended to

Liberia to assist her in developing a viable economy, but
with the additional constraint that the assistance neither be
given nor used in such a way that it appears to make Liberia
a United States puppet. This new complication must be kept
firmly in mind when evaluating recent United States aid
activities in Liberia, since, rightly or wrongly, it is a criterion against which others will judge United States economic
development efforts in Africa.

UNITED STATES ECONOMIC AID 1940-1950

The history of external aid to Liberia may be divided into
two periods, the separation date being 1951. Prior to that
year, all external aid came from the United States, was given
without a formal program, and was applied to the Liberian
economy without the aid of either an economic development
plan or a planning organization. Subsequent to 1951, all of
these characteristics have been significantly altered.

Lend Lease

On March 31, 1942, the United States and Liberia concluded
the Defense Areas Agreement which permitted the basing of
United States Military personnel in Liberia. Under this
agreement, the United States received the right to control,
operate and defend airports and all installations necessary to
their efficient operation, including the construction of access
roads--one from Monrovia to Roberts Field, and one from
Monrovia to Fisherman's Lake. The former road was completed, and still continues to be the main highway linking the
capital with the interior. Work on the road to Fisherman's
Lake was discontinued when Roberts Field was sufficiently
enlarged to handle all air traffic. On June 8, 1943, Lend
Lease was formally extended to Liberia, the total credits
extended amounting to $496,000. The cost of other activities
such as Roberts Field and roads remains secreted in the
mysteries of Department of Defense financial records.

Roberts Field

At the close of World War II, United States Army personnel

were withdrawn from Roberts Field, despite State Department objections to the closing of the facility. [2] Shortly
thereafter, a private United States company was formed with
the purpose of managing the field and using it for freight
service between the United States and Liberia. However,
pressure was brought on the Liberian Government by the
Liberia Company which culminated in the granting of management rights to Pan American Airways Corporation, in
return for which this company agreed to provide bi-weekly
scheduled service between Liberia and the United States. The
airfield has been subsequently enlarged to accomodate jet
planes, but further development and expansion are urgently
required in the interests of safety. Pan American also
conducts a training program for Liberian ground personnel
which contributes to the nation's supply of skilled labor.

Highway Construction

Construction of the Monrovia-Ganta road was initiated by
the United States Army and completed by the Liberia Construction Company through a grant from the United States.
In 1942, the trip from the capital to Ganta was measured in
terms of weeks, whereas it now may be made in five hours.
The traveler observes along the road a congregation of
people far in excess of the average population density for the
country as a whole. Cash crop production, such as rubber
and coffee, has almost completely replaced the traditional
village farm along the entire stretch of the highway. In
addition, people living within the influence of the road have
been brought into much closer political contact with Monrovia, a development of undeniable importance to the central
government.

Free Port of Monrovia

United States interest in establishing a naval base at Monrovia dates back to 1909. [3] However, it was not until President Roosevelt visited President King in 1942 that a firm
commitment to build a port was made to Liberia. Under the
final agreement, technical responsibility for the project was
given to the U.S. Navy Department. For both practical and
legal reasons, however, the Navy did not undertake the

actual construction.   Raymond Pile and Concrete Company,
a private United States firm, was engaged by the Liberian
Government and work began in 1945. [4]

The financing of the Port was a case of history almost
repeating itself, with the difference being that the second
venture was a success.   President Woodrow Wilson attempted
to use his war powers in 1919 to make a $5 million loan to
Liberia.   The negotiations became so protracted that the
presidential powers expired before the arrangements were
concluded, at which time the project was dropped.   President
Roosevelt used Lend Lease as the vehicle to provide the
funds; a $19 million credit was extended to Liberia under the
Mutual Aid Agreement of 1943.   In addition to the port proper
the project provided for an access road and bridge over the
St. Paul River.   This facility made it convenient to later
establish rail connections between Bomi Hills and the Port.
Without this installation, Lansdell Christie's development of
the Bomi Hills iron ore deposit would have been jeopardized.
Assured of the vital rail connection, LMC was able to pro-
ceed rapidly with its project, and made its first ore shipment in 1952.

Under the terms of the agreement, the Port is designated
as a Free Port, which means that merchandise can be
landed, stored, processed and reshipped to other countries
without payment of import duty.   Article 5 of the Agreement
provides for an American corporation to manage the port
during the period of amortization of the loan.   Having the
most vital interest in the port at this time, Mr. Christie,
president of LMC, took the leadership in promoting the formation of the Monrovia Port Management Company having the
following stock holders:
  Farrell Lines Corporation
  Mississippi Shipping Company
  Socony-Vacuum Oil Company
  The Texas Company
  Liberia Mining Company
  Firestone Plantations Company
  Republic of Liberia
Each stockholder has one representative on the board except
the Republic of Liberia which has two.   The company is
responsible for publishing rules and regulations and tariffs of
fees and charges.   It is required to employ Liberians and

train them whenever possible. A management fee of 5 per
cent of gross revenues was to be paid to the company until
1953, which increased to 10 per cent thereafter. After
meeting operating expenses and providing for improvement,
the company is to remit the balance of income to the Liberian Government for transfer to the United States for amortization of the original cost. Between 1949 and 1953, total
tonnage increased from 94,500 to 1 million gross tons.
Gross revenues rose from $292,400 to $600,000, and net
income increased from $100,000 to $160,000. The use of the
Port, measured by revenues, increased steadily, albeit
slowly, until 1959 when gross revenue increased by 27 per
cent over 1958. A further rise of 39 per cent occurred in
1960. Net revenues have not shown the same trend, however.
Profit declined in 1959 compared to 1958, but rose by 50 per
cent between 1959 and 1960. So far, the Port Management
Company has been able to make additional investment in new
and expanded facilities, but it is not clear whether adequate
provision has been made for depreciation and interest
charges. The Port Agreement provides for the credit to be
non-interest bearing, but it has been the policy of the United
States to consider this feature as a foreign assistance grant
to Liberia and not an advantage to be passed on to the users
of the Port in the form of lower rates. During the period
1958 to 1962 the outstanding amount of the original credit
was slightly under $19 million. At an interest rate of 3 per
cent, the annual interest charge on this principal would be
$570,000. It is apparent from Table 19 that earnings so far
have not been sufficient to cover this cost. Two major
studies of the Port operation, one made in 1954 and the other
in 1962, both find that fees and charges are below those for
similar facilities in West Africa. [5] With an annual rate of
return on the original investment less than 2 per cent, it
seems reasonable to argue that the Port users are being
subsidized by the United States Government.

The United States and the Republic of Liberia concluded
in 1965 an agreement which will transfer the Port to Liberian ownership with a graduated rate of amortization of the
outstanding debt of $18.9 million through 1999. The annual
payments will be placed in an education foundation to be
jointly administered by Liberia and the United States. It is
expected that when this transfer of ownership is complete,

Liberia will establish a national Port Authority to administer
all port facilities. At this time, it is highly probably that
tariffs will be raised which will increase net revenues. This
last expectation is based on the assumption that the demand
for port services is inelastic, especially since fees are
below those of other West African ports. It is to be hoped
that Liberia will retain a professional management organization having broad administrative powers, and will recognize
that adequate depreciation plus expansion and modernization
must take a first claim on earnings.

Table 19: Financial Operations of the Free Port of
　　　　　　Monrovia--Selected Years (thousands of dollars)

Year	Gross Revenue	Operating Expenses	Net Revenue
1949	292	192	100
1953	600	440	160
1958	987	742	245
1959	1,241	1,066	175
1960	1,720	1,454	266
1961	2,369	2,020	349
1962	2,682	2,199	483

Source: Sly and Heddon, The Free Port and Harbor of Monrovia, p. 11, and Office of National Planning, Republic of
Liberia.

Liberia Mining Company Loan

    In the preceding section, note was taken of the invaluable
contribution made by the Port of Monrovia to the iron ore
mining venture of Lansdell K. Christie at Bomi Hills. The
original expectation of Mr. Christie was to build a railroad
from the port to the mine site, to establish mining operations,
and then to expand gradually the operation as income was
received from the sale of ore. Before actual mining operations could be started, financial difficulties necessitated the
acquisition of additional capital. Mr. Christie turned to two
sources--Republic Steel Corporation and the Export-Import
Bank of Washington. Republic Steel purchased an undisclosed

amount of common stock, reputedly amounting to about one-half interest in the company. The Export-Import Bank undertook to loan $4 million for ten years to the company for the purpose of building the necessary railroad from the mine site to the Port. This loan was made in 1949, and by 1953 it had been completely retired. [6]

TECHNICAL ASSISTANCE 1944-1950

Origin and Purpose

The roads and other projects developed by the United States Army personnel in Liberia during World War II, the financing of the Port of Monrovia, and the Liberia Mining Company Loan were the principal United States public capital investments in Liberia during the decade 1940-1950. From these activities stemmed the two technical assistance missions operative in Liberia between 1944 and 1950. One of these was the United States Economic Mission of the Foreign Economic Administration, and the other was the United States Public Health Mission in Liberia. These missions were administratively separate organizations, and both were ad hoc bodies controlled by different United States Government agencies. In 1950, however, their activities were integrated and placed on a more permanent footing by establishing the Joint United States-Liberia Economic Commission authorized in the 1950 Act for International Development.

The Port Agreement of 1944 provided for a United States Economic Mission which would survey the economic potential of Liberia. The purposes of the Economic Mission have been described by Dr. Earl Parker Hanson, the first head of the mission, as follows:[7]

1. The study and screening of Liberia's import requirements as prepared by the Liberian Government, and the subsequent advising of the United States on the country's relative needs for various items as interpreted by (the mission).

2. The survey of Liberia's resources, and the evaluation of all of these resources that may come to play a part in

future development.

3. The preparation of proposals to the Liberian Government and (the United States Government), for specific
lines of endeavor which would further economic development.

The first of these functions was a routine war-time
activity, inasmuch as Liberian import requirements for
economic development had to be evaluated as to essentiality,
because of war-caused scarcities of goods in the United
States. The conduct of surveys and drafting of proposals for
developmental projects were more fundamental and lasting
functions.

The United States Public Health Mission in Liberia was
an outgrowth of concern by United States Army doctors over
what they regarded as the appalling medical and health conditions then existing in Liberia. This concern was heightened
when it was decided to build the port, which meant that Amer-
can civilian personnel would be living in the Monrovia area.
Malaria was rampant, especially in and around Monrovia and
constituted the most important health problem. Enteric
diseases ranked second in importance, and many other tropical diseases, about which little was known, were found
widespread. The American Envoy to Liberia was instructed
to propose to President William V. S. Tubman that a public
health mission be sent to Liberia. The President formally
requested the Mission with the proviso that Major John B.
West of the United States Public Health Service be made its
leader. This request was honored and the Mission was
established in 1944. [8]

As the work of the Public Health and Economic Mission
progressed, a second function gradually came to assume a
position of paramount importance. This new purpose was the
drafting, through the coordinated efforts of the two missions
and the Liberian Government, of a long-range plan for
Liberia's economic development. This activity represented a
subtle shift in the purpose and concept of these missions.
Gradually, the role of technical assistance missions in planning and executing economic development programs became
accepted as a permanent part of Liberian economic life.

Major Activities

Forestry Survey

The forestry resources of Liberia had for some time been regarded as a major source of income to the country. The first attempt to conduct a complete survey of this resource was undertaken by the Economic Mission during the years 1947 and 1949. The findings of this survey are summarized in Mr. Mayer's report. [9] The report included a recommended forest exploitation plan involving an investment in saw mills of $3.2 million. Unfortunately, this proposal was never implemented by either private or public capital.

Geological Survey

The geological investigations made by the Economic Mission were limited in scope, the principal work in this field being accomplished after 1951 by the Joint Commission. The first study conducted by the Economic Mission was of iron ore deposits in the Bomi Hills area. However, soon after the mission team began to survey this deposit, the lease agreement between the Liberia Mining Company and the Government of Liberia was signed, whereupon the mission withdrew from the survey except to render consultation service and technical advice to the Liberian Government. The mission geologists made innumerable field trips, collected and evaluated samples of various mineral resources, and prepared maps of all of the surveyed areas.

Agriculture

The forestry and geological programs were largely a process of inventory taking and cataloging of results and findings. The agriculture program, while being primarily confined to surveys, permitted a considerable amount of direct contact between mission personnel and Liberians in all parts of the country. As a result, a substantial amount of assistance relating to day-to-day farm problems was given to farmers by the mission specialists. Unlike the immutable data of forestry or mineral reserves as of a given date, the agricultural potential of a country can be discovered only by experimentation and testing of new crops and

methods in the field. Because the study of soil problems
and crop experimentation required close association between
the technicians and the Liberian farmers, the latter became
the direct recipients of a considerable amount of direct technical assistance.

The activities of the agricultural technicians were numerous and varied. An effort was made to strengthen the Department of Agriculure, field surveys were conducted, seeds,
fertilizers and other supplies were both employed at demonstration centers and sold to farmers at cost, and the nucleus
of an extension program was inaugurated. The most intensive program was the Dimeh-Amino project which was directed
toward modifying of the total cultural pattern of that area in
order to increase food and cash crop production. This project
was regionally, rather than functionally, oriented; and it
involved both agricultural specialists and public health experts.
As such, the Dimeh-Amino project helped to set the stage for
the later Rural Area Development project at Gbarnga. An
important lesson learned from this exercise was that the African will accept new ideas and changes when he can be shown
that they improve on what he has.

The agriculture program of the Economic Mission and
especially its work at the experimental centers pointed up the
need for long-range study of many problems, such as plant
diseases and the use of sprays, insecticides and fertilizers.
Such a research program required trained technicians, which
Liberia was then unable to supply. Agricultural extension
work required that other fields of development be coordinated
with agricultural development if the latter was to be successfully
pursued. One of the most pressing needs was transportation,
particularly roads, which required not only technical assistance but physical capital as well. At the village level, agricultural changes had to be supplemented with programs in
simple health and hygiene practices, as well as fundamental
education in literacy, handicrafts and other skills.

Civil Engineering Surveys

This phase of the mission activities was directed primarily
to transportation, communications and power development. A
noteworthy task was the serial photographing of practically all
of Liberia which later permitted the construction of the first

authoritative maps and relief mosaics of the country. The
mission engineers carried on reconnaissance surveys for
railroads, coastal and inland shipping, and a network of motor
roads. These surveys included the mapping of routes, plans
for improvement of existing roads, trials, and bridges. A
team of specialists from the United States Department of the
Interior studied the possible construction of hydro-electric
plants. One proposal of this study team was for a hydro
plant to be built on the St. Paul River, a project which is
currently under construction.

Public Health Programs

The first project of the Public Health Mission was an
attack upon malaria in Monrovia. A DDT spraying was
accomplished with the assistance of Liberian personnel,
trained in spraying at Roberts Field. The result of this spraying was a drop within one year of malaria incidence of 95 per
cent.[10] Other diseases, such as helminthiasis and venereal
diseases, were found to respond well to treatment by the then
new sulfa drugs.

These initial results, while phenomenal on the surface, were
of little or no permanent importance. Malaria control requires
continuous effort and at times large capital outlays to effectively and permanently drain swamps and breeding places. Of
equal importance is training of doctors and nurses and equip-
ping them to combat effectively the many ills and diseases.
Establishing an effective preventive, rather than a solely
curative, program is the ultimate public health goal. Achieving
this objective requires a many-sided program which includes
training of professional and sub-professional medical personnel, establishing clinics throughout the country, improving the
diet, and breaking down of aboriginal resistance to modern
medical techniques.

During the tenure of the Public Health Mission the following
steps toward improved health conditions were taken:

1. Liberian expenditures on health rose from $72,000 in
1944 to $442,000 in 1950.

2. A public health information service was initiated in the
schools.

3. A curriculum for nurse and medical technician training was developed, which formed the basis of the Tubman National Institute of Medical Arts, established in 1952.

A reduction in the size of the mission began in late 1948 in anticipation of its dissolution on June 30, 1949. From this latter date until the creation of the Joint Commission in 1951, no formal technical assistance was given to Liberia in the public health field. While only a very small dent was made in the overwhelming health problems of Liberia, the mission paved the way for instituting a long-range, comprehensive public health program in Liberia.

Other Projects

The Economic Mission also conducted surveys of small business opportunities under conditions of local material, capital, and skill resources, a survey of palm oil possibilities, special education studies, and an intensive survey of the Liberian fiscal system.[11] Some of these recommendations were adopted either in whole or in part. Most, however, met the fate of many such reports which is to languish unread on dusty shelves, only to be duplicated years later when the original study is forgotten or is out-of-date.

As incomplete as many of the surveys were, they did provide some data about parts of the Liberian economy heretofore unknown. Most significant, perhaps, was the realization that statistics are either available or collectable if only one has the modest resources and the deep interest necessary to assemble them.

NATIONAL ECONOMIC PLANNING

Early Planning Efforts

The activities of the Economic Mission and the Public Health Mission between 1944 and 1950 were viewed by Liberian officials as supplementing the development plan of that country. In 1944, however, no plan existed in the current meaning of this term, as applied to underdeveloped areas.

What passed for a development plan was nothing more than a set of thirteen points which represented the basic economic and political objectives of the Tubman Administration. Among these proposed areas of action were proposals for a diversified educational system, a health and sanitation education program, the encouragement and protection of domestic and foreign investment, the development of transportation and communication facilities, surveys of agricultural, mining and other natural resources, and the encouragement of immigration. [12]

The Development Plan of 1946 was drafted on the basis of a request by the United States embodied in the Port Agreement. The result was a series of projects grouped under broad titles of construction, agriculture, natural resources, industry, research and product development, education, public health, banking, and non-economic programs such as the extension of universal sufferage and changes in hinterland administration. The estimated cost of the entire program was $25 million, and it was to be financed by a fifty year loan with amortization to begin after five years. This was a bold proposal considering that the Liberian budget had, at that time, never exceeded $1.8 million. At 3 per cent per annum, interest charges alone would have cost the Government $750,000 annually until amortization payments began.

As a planning document, the Development Plan of 1946 left much to be desired. The Plan evaded the controversial and fundamental issue of political reform in Liberia. There was no financial plan devised to supplement the project proposals. The success of the Plan seemed to hinge upon certain contingencies, such as the continuation and possible expansion of United States technical and economic assistance, increased private foreign investment, and an expansion of government revenues. The proposed plan revealed that technically competent people are as necessary to draft a plan as they are to put it into operation. Not only are specialists in various program fields necessary to formulate a workable development plan, but financial and administration technicians are also required. Furthermore, economic planning must be predicated upon a minimum amount of factual knowledge. A rational allocation of economic resources is unlikely if there exists no notion of the quantity, quality and location of these resources, the potential uses to which they may be put, and the character of

local as well as world markets for the products.[13] Moreover, the Plan failed to indicate an awareness on the part of
the planners of the need for taking a realistic view of political and social impediments to economic development.
Refusal to consider these problems for whatever reason, may
cause the plan to be abortive. Finally, a plan should contain
some means of effectively measuring accomplishments. The
only such test in the Liberian plan was the number of physical
projects completed. The nearest thing to an economic
measure of fulfillment was the statement that the legislature
had adopted the "following five-year plan for the over-all
development of the Republic. "

This planning endeavor was never to become operative,
and it was finally superseded by a revised plan in 1951.

The Five Year Economic Development Plan of 1951
envisaged a series of projects in five major areas, as
follows:

Government Administration	$ 1,193,000
Agriculture	4,226,430
Engineering	11,267,260
Public Health	8,773,000
Education	7,120,040
Total	$32,579,730

The most important innovation of this plan was the establishment of the Joint United States-Liberian Commission for
Economic Development (the Joint Commission) consisting of
seven Liberian Cabinet Ministers and six United States AID
Mission representatives. The Joint Commission had a Liberian
administrative secretary and a staff of clerical workers. No
professional economic or planning personnel were authorized
for, or utilized by, the Joint Commission. The functions of the
Joint Commission were to:

1. Allocate funds and technical personnel to the various
agencies to carry out assigned projects.

2. Draft specifications and construction or operational
contracts and provide contractors.

3. Make progress inspections of construction work on
other operations carried out with development program

funds.

4. Determine the timing and completion date of each project.

5. Prepare loan applications for submission to the Liberian Government, where loans are deemed necessary to finance particular projects.

6. Give special consideration to the interests of private investors in order to encourage their participation in the national development plan.

The $32. 6 million necessary to finance the plan was to come from current Government revenues, grants-in-aid from the United States and the United Nations specialized agencies, and loans from public and private external sources. These financial proposals were a distinct improvement over the financing arrangements suggested in the Plan of 1946. Instead of relying entirely upon foreign loans, this plan established a minimum sum to be supplied from internal sources, and which was made dependent upon the size of the total budget. This proposal reflected the official United States opinion that "we anticipate that a large part of the financing of new capital will be obtained in the developing country itself." [14] The President of Liberia concurred in principle with the proposed development financing, stating that Liberia will never possess the things she wants "if we expect them to be the free gifts of others, and I am sure that no Liberian desires or expects gifts of this kind." [15]

The Five Year Plan of 1951 improved on its predecessors by providing for a permanent and responsible administrative body, by incorporating within the plan a financing program based upon internal revenues which would be generated by economic development, by establishing a target date, and by utilizing technical experts to draft the plan. Its shortcomings, as revealed by experience, were many. The projects were not coordinated within the framework of a total set of objectives and an all-embracing development strategy. The plan failed to provide effective guidelines for the setting of either inter- or intra-sectoral priorities, with the consequence that the projects which received approval were, by and

large, those which were given first consideration. Despite
the fact that United Nations and other public as well as
private sources of assistance were to play a major role in
the implementation of the plan, administration and decision
making power rested solely with the Joint Commission--a
Liberian-American body. Some of the subsequent misunderstandings which arose between Point Four Administrators
and private investors may be traced to this lack of formal
means of coordinating their efforts.

In 1955, the Economic Plan was revised and extended
until 1959. Titled "The Extended Five-Year Development
Plan," this plan was merely an amplification of the same project areas of the 1951 Plan with a $71. 8 million price tag.
The major alteration was an increase in the relative allot-
ment to public works from 35 to 71 per cent, and a propor-
tionate reduction in the relative allocations to other sectors.
Some shift in emphasis occurred within sectors, most
notably a swing toward adult and vocational education at the
expense of rural and elementary education. Finance proposals remained substantially unchanged, and the Joint Commission continued as both a policy-making and administrative
body.

National Planning Agency

The most glaring difficulty inherent in these early plans
was the nature and composition of the planning organization.
Because the members were department secretaries and
their principal United States advisors, the criterion for success for each member became the advancement of his department's program rather than the advancement of the economy
as a whole. Where these two objectives coincided, all was
well. In the case of a conflict between the department's
growth and that of the economy, such as a proposed cut-back
of a particular program to allow one in another department to
expand, it was the departmental orientation which generally
controlled the members' position. Thus, departmental projects and programs were viewed more as competitors for
available resources rather than as elements of a single
coordinated national plan. Reconciliation of such rivalries
led to the adoption of two forms of compromise. A certain
amount of mutual "back scratching" was one. When deadlocks

over priorities continued to arise, the second method of
resolving disagreement--referring the matter to the President for a decision--was employed. Neither of these methods
proved satisfactory, inasmuch as both led to decisons
which were based more on political expediency than on
economic soundness.

Compounding these difficulties was the inherent structure
of the Joint Commission which caused it to serve simul-
taneously as planner, executor and evaluator of projects.
This breach of approved organizational structure has made an
independent impartial evaluation of performance difficult, if
not impossible. Since 1960, the country has had no formal
plan and while foreign aid continues to be nominally administered by the Joint Commission, the projects have been
planned and executed on an ad hoc basis. In addition, the
United States has accelerated its activities in the areas of
health, education, and agriculture. While these programs are
taken into consideration by the Joint Commission, the fact that
the United Nations is not represented in the planning body has
led to the making of informal bilateral agreements between
operating departments and the U. N. In all such cases, the
final approval of the President continues to be necessary to
formalize these programs, but since there exists neither a
master plan against which the individual projects may be
measured nor provision for professional and independent
evaluation of alternatives, inevitable duplication has occurred
in some areas along with uncovered gaps in others. This
criticism does not imply that each and every sector should
receive equal attention at the same time. Planning inherently
means that some programs and projects are being deferred at
the same time that others are receiving a higher priority.
But choices between alternatives both at a given point of time
and between time periods are ideally made with the object of
maximizing the national welfare.

The principal difficulty throughout the entire period of
planning in Liberia has been the failure of planning and
administrative officials to distinguish between a plan as a
document and as a process for establishing goals, strategies,
and priorities, and enforcing adherence to them. This failure
became patently evident in 1961 when the President of Liberia
presented, on the occasion of a state visit to the United States,
a "plan" consisting of a $400 million project shopping

list. For the most part, this proposal was a summation of
individual department plans, many of them hastily drawn and
being neither internally consistent nor coordinated with other
facets of the economy.

The Liberian President was reminded of his statement
made in 1960 to the effect that administrative reforms were
necessary in his Government. The United States proposed
that a national comprehensive development plan be formulated
by a process which secured the participation and cooperation
of all units of government as well as all facets of the private
economy. The first step taken in this direction was the
establishment on May 8, 1962, of the National Planning
Agency along lines recommended by Mr. Gerhard Colm. The
NPA consists of two arms, the National Planning Council with
the President as chairman and six cabinet ministers as members; and the Office of National Planning under a Director-
General who has cabinet rank and who also serves as Executive Secretary of the NPC. The agency is to coordinate all
government programs which involve production of goods and
services, foreign assistance programs, foreign private
investment projects, and the well-being of the people. The
NPC is the policy-making branch for which the ONP provides
professional and technical staff support. The plan also
provides that each operating department appoint a Program
Planning Officer, each of whom will coordinate departmental
project development and serve as a liaison between the department and the ONP.

To date, the NPA has not produced a document titled
"Economic Development Plan" although it has, with the
assistance of the United States and the United Nations, made
considerable strides in laying the basis for an effective planning process. [16] While the planning organization represents
improvement over the planning process of the past, it retains
features of the past which then, as now, mitigate against
achieving optimal results. The basic policy decisions by law,
and most operating decisions in practice, rest with a body of
cabinet ministers and ultimately with the President. While
basic economic policy-making is properly a political matter,
the formulation of a comprehensive set of criteria and priorities within the broad confines of executive policy should be
left to planning experts who are divorced from inter-depart-
mental jealousies and rivalries. With many of the people

sitting on the NPC having been members of the Joint Commission, it is difficult to quickly break down a modus
operandi which became institutionalized under the Joint Commission.   The Director-General has been found to spend too
much of his time on these matters with the result that far too
little of his limited resources has been free to perform the
assigned job of the organization.   Nevertheless, this had to
be done in order to gain acceptance of the Planning Agency by
the rest of the Government.   The pessimists feel that breaking
through a century of established decision-making practice in
Liberia will not be possible for a very long time, if ever.   In
the view of these critics, the NPA will provide a sufficient
facade of vigorous planning activity to permit the Government
to be fashionable, but decisions will continue to be made in
the same ad hoc manner as in the past.   Others are cautiously
optimistic, believing that, given appropriate personnel shifts,
the inexorable pressures of national economic development
and possibly those arising from international planning and
project operation alliances, will force the Government to use
the NPA as its primary economic decision maker.

EXTERNAL ASSISTANCE 1951-1964

During the period between 1951 and 1964, foreign economic
assistance to Liberia expanded both by amount and by source
of funds.   The United States was the principal supplier of
both technical assistance and loans, followed by the Federal
Republic of Germany and the United Nations (see Table 20).
The United Nations Program, while less than that of Germany
in amount, dates back to 1951.   The International Bank for
Reconstruction and Development was utilized only once during
this period, and the International Monetary Fund supplied a
stand-by credit for monetary stabilization purposes.   The
United Kingdom, Israel, China, Sweden, Yugoslavia and the
Vatican have also given or extended an offer of aid.   Most of
these forms of assistance have taken the form of scholarships,
individual technicians, or grants to construct a particular
capital project such as a medical training center (Vatican) or a
slaughter house (Yugoslavia).

The remainder of this chapter will deal primarily with
United States economic assistance since this country has
been the principal supplier of public funds. Also, through
its membership on the Joint Commission, the United States
has exerted considerable influence upon the determination of
project and sector priorities. United Nations technical
assistance and loans and aid from others have followed these
leads, filling obvious gaps and strengthening other areas of
concern.

Table 20: Principal Sources & Forms of Foreign Economic
           Assistance to Liberia, 1942-64 (millions of
           dollars)

Donor or Lender	Total	Technical Assistance	Loans
United States:			
1942-1950	27. 5	3. 5	24. 0
1951-1964	166. 2*	49. 4	116.8 **
United Nations	5. 7	5. 7	--
Federal Republic of Germany	13. 5	1. 0	12. 5
IBRD	3. 25	--	3. 25
IMF	8. 4	--	8. 4

 * Includes Military assistance of $5.1 million and Public Law
    480 loans of $2.4 million, but excludes Peace Corps.
** Includes loans committed but unsigned as of June 30, 1964,
    of $38.7 million.

Source: Office of National Planning, Annual Reports

Pattern of Technical Assistance

United States technical assistance to Liberia has embraced
several major areas of activity. Significant changes, however,
have taken place in the relative importance of particular

sectors over time. The sharp upward movement of allot-
ments to education in 1962 reflects the shift in U. S. aid philosophy in favor of investment in human resources promulgated in
the Foreign Assistance Act of 1961. A similar expansion took
place in the public administration sector, partly because of
the same philosophical change which led to increased education expenditures, and partly as a result of a shift in the
attitude of the Liberian Government toward the matter of
government reform. On the other hand, expenditures for
public health have declined in recent years. Presently this
program is in a state of transition from a curative to a medical training orientation. Most of the work currently under
way in the curative area such as malaria prevention, small-
pox, yaws and intestinal parasite eradication is being conducted by the Government of Liberia with the assistance of the
World Health Organization. Some of the reasons for the
decline in agriculture assistance will be discussed later. Community development activities commanded the largest share of
funds in 1951, but declined to a token expenditure by 1956.
Beginning in 1962, renewed effort in this area was centered on
the Rural Area Development (RAD) project in Gbarnga. Unfortunately the data do not   indicate the total amount allocated to
this program as some of the RAD funds are included in other
expenditure categories.

Loan Assistance

Since 1951, United States loan assistance to Liberia has
totaled $116. 8 million, including loans committed as of June,
1964. In 1965, an additional $9. 9 million was committed for
the construction of a sewerage plant in Monrovia. Loans from
other public sources since 1955 have totaled $24. 4 million,
bringing the total of foreign public loans to $151 million
including the sewerage system loan. The loans have been distributed among the major sectors of the economy as follows:

Electric power	$ 36. 4 million	
Iron Ore Mining	40. 5	"
Medical facilities	5. 3	"
Education facilities	2. 1	"
Water and Sewer	18. 3	"
Roads and Airports	34. 6	"
Monetary Stability	8. 4	"

| General Development | 5.5 million |
| TOTAL | $ 151.1 million |

About 40 per cent of this total are credits which have been
extended or committed since 1963 and the bulk of these have
not yet been expended. In addition, $40.5 million of United
States loans was to private iron ore mining companies.
Thus the total of such loans actually spent to date on governmental projects is about $50 million. Offsetting these
adjustments is the borrowing of more than $86 million by the
Government of Liberia in private capital markets plus
development projects financed directly from current revenues. It is further estimated that 4 per cent of the annual
budget was allocated to capital projects during the period
under review which implies an expenditure for capital projects of $11-$12 million from this source. Thus, the total
publically financed capital investment over this fourteen year
period totals $137 million, or just under an average of $10
million per year. However, as in the case of private capital
inflow, this expenditure has not proceeded at a steady rate.
Most of the public loan funds and all of the privately borrowed
capital have been expended or committed since 1959.

Major Foreign Assistance Activities

Although technical assistance and loan assistance are
statistically separable, they are functionally indivisible
Some distinction between them may be made on grounds that
technical aid has been concentrated in the area of human
resource development while loan assistance has been mainly
utilized for infrastructure creation, such as highways and
school buildings. An input-output matrix, however, would
readily reveal the interdependence of these artificially defined
categories of foreign aid. Increased agricultural production
requires technical knowledge, but its realization also demands
roads and marketing facilities. Effective education is more
than a log with a student at one end and the teacher at the
other. Buildings, supplies, and equipment must complement
the teacher. A proper evaluation of that impact of foreign
aid on an economy requires that the assistance be viewed within the framework of the total economy which includes foreign
private investment and domestic economic

activity.   To make such an evaluation of foreign aid to the
Liberian economy would require much more refined data than
is presently available.   A second best approach is to describe
selected activities against the background of the general framework of the economy presented in Chapter 1.   The areas
selected for particular treatment are education, agriculture,
public administration and infrastructure investment.

Table 21:   United States Technical Assistance to Liberia by
Field of Activity (selected years)
(Thousands of U.S. Dollars)

Activity	1951	1956	1960	1961	1962	1963	1964
Total	827[1]	1782	2760	3050	10660	8550	6020
Agriculture	44	304	420	480	640	--	250
Industry, Mining and Labor	--	112	--	10	50	--	480
Health and Sanitation	192	324	120	110	630	270	170
Education	43	558	670	370	4000	3470	1680
Transportation and Communication	--	255	280	370	240	60	--
Public Admin.	--	28	490	550	3100	2330	2130
Public Safety	--	--	--	270	150	550	370
General and Community Development	395	30	780	890	850	1870	940
Other	153[2]	161	--	--	--	--	--

1- Authorized Amounts, Obligations for which breakdown by
field of activity was not available were $774,000 for 1951.
2- Continuation of Aerial Mapping Program of United States
Economic Mission .

Source: Republic of Liberia, Bureau of Audits, Annual Reports
United States State Department, Post-War Economic Aid to
Africa, 1944 - 1952, p. 36.   United States Senate, Development
of Technical Assistance Programs, pp. 110-115.   Agency for
International Development, unpublished data.

Education

    In 1951 the status of education in Liberia might have been
described as appalling. No branch or level of education--
elementary, secondary, university or vocational--compared
favorably with its counterpart in other African territories.
For this reason, no single educational problem stood out
above others as being paramount. Furthermore, these problems were interdependent, and the solution of one necessitated
a simultaneous attack upon all others. Nevertheless, finances
and personnel limitations made it impossible to launch a
frontal attack upon all aspects of education. The procedure,
therefore, has been to single out for attack particularly strategic areas. Five programs have constituted the core of the
Liberian attack upon the education problem. They are: (1)
improvement of administration and supervision, (2) development of a teacher training program, (3) creation of a rural
educational program, (4) expansion and improvement of vocational education, and (5) upgrading of higher and professional
education.

Table 22:   United Nations Technical Assistance to Liberia--
            1963-64 (Thousands of dollars)

Agency	1963	1964
UNTA	54	43
ILO	27	36
FAO	117	45
UNESCO	32	27
ICAO	38	49
WHO	74	61
Others	30	30
TOTAL	372	291

Plus aid from Special Funds for which no amounts are
specified, but which is probably in excess of $7,000,000.

Source: Office of National Planning, Annual Report, 1962-1963
(Monrovia: 1963).

Only a sample of the innumerable sub-projects which have been undertaken in the general area of administration may be presented. The organization of the Department of Education has been streamlined by joint action of the Education Department, USAID, and Special Commission on Government Organization (SCOGO) personnel. A uniform pupil accounting and record system has been made which gives the Department for the first time a complete and accurate record of the number and location of schools, teachers and pupils. A Teachers' Salary, Tenure and Retirement Act was drafted and enacted in 1956. Since 1962, a team from San Francisco State College has been creating the institutional and legal framework for a Monrovia Consolidated School System, which when implemented will immeasurably improve the administration and teaching efforts in Monrovia schools. United States capital assistance to the Monrovia school project includes a $1.7 million loan for a Junior-Senior high school and a $350,000 loan for an elementary school plus supplies and equipment.

The teacher training program has continuously occupied a central position in the United States' aid program. The teacher supply problem has both quantitative and qualitative dimensions. Not only have the number of teachers not kept pace with the growth of student enrollment but the level of preparation, which was initially low, has tended to deteriorate under the pressure of increased demand. Between 1946 and 1963 the total number of teachers in elementary and secondary schools increased from 569 to 2158, or 3.8 times. During the same time period, the number of students rose from 12,000 to 68,500, a 5.7-fold increase. The consequences of this disproportionate expansion in the number of teachers and students have been larger classes, less qualified teachers, and lower quality education. In 1963, 54 per cent of all government schools had a pupil-teacher ratio of 30:1 or more, 33 per cent had a ratio of 40:1 or higher, and 20 per cent had 50 or more students per teacher. In the same year, 4 per cent of government school teachers had completed less than 8th grade, 44 per cent had finished less than 10th grade, and 69 per cent had received less than 12 years of formal education. Finally, the drop-out rate in Monrovia was 70 per cent of students by the third grade.

The key to the remedy for this condition is believed to lie

with the quality of teachers. When attempts to upgrade teachers through the use of summer workshops and training classes proved to be incapable of offsetting the deterioration of quality which was taking place, a more concerted attack upon the problem was launched in the early 1960's. This approach culminated in the activation of Rural Teacher Training Institutes at Zorzor and Kakata. The RTTI curriculum is a two year course of study designed to raise the educational level of teachers who had nine or ten years of schooling up to a high school graduate level. The first institute was established at Zorzor with the assistance of a team from Tuskegee Institute, financed by the United States along with most of the plant construction costs. The Zorzor Institute began operation in 1963 and graduated its first class in 1964. A second institute was opened at Kakata in 1964 and its first graduation class will leave in 1965. The success of this program required that teachers who attended the institutes for two years be replaced for this period. The Peace Corps has provided more than three hundred teachers, most of whom are filling this role. Partly because of this cooperative effort of two aiding agencies, the Rural Teachers Institute program promises to be one of the most successful of all education programs in Liberia.

Rural and adult education projects have been assisted by both the United States and UNESCO. In October, 1954, a rural education specialist was assigned to the United States Operations Mission in Liberia, under whose guidance a rural elementary education curriculum for rural areas was devised and implemented in cooperation with the Department of Agriculture and Commerce and the National Public Health Service. The basic philosophy of the rural education program has been that the rural school should become the community center, providing not only formal education but also other services which affect the social and economic life of the whole community. In 1962, USAID undertook to build twenty rural schools in the Gbarnga area as part of the rural area development program. Ten additional schools are planned for both the Voinjama and Sannequellie districts.

The UNESCO contribution to rural education is centered in the Fundamental Educational Center at Klay which began in 1951 as a field project and became a training center in 1954. UNESCO workers are reluctant to give a formal definition to fundamental education. Its content,they believe, must be determined by conditions of time and place. The basic ingredients are literacy training, instruction in basic agricultural, public health, and sanitation techniques. Students at Klay receive instruction in English, sanitation, elementary meteorology, literacy and adult education methods, arithmetic, child care, first aid, history and agricultural theory and practice. Upon graduation, these students return to their villages to teach by example, and by formal classes if requested by the villagers. [17]

The only operating vocational education school in Liberia prior to 1964 was Booker Washington Institute. The school was established in 1928 by Dr. James L. Sibley with the aid of a grant from the Phelps-Stokes Foundation. Ownership and responsibility were ceded to the Liberian Government in 1953. Since that date, United States technicians have been active in both building the curriculum and teaching classes. The curriculum consists of academic high school subjects along with training programs in agriculture, metal working, automobile mechanics, business training, home economics, and radio and electrical training. In 1963, the school had a total enrollment of 514 students, 62 of which were seniors. It presently has a capacity of 600 students, and no further expansion is visualized for the near future. A high percentage of BWI graduates go on to further education at the university level. While the country gains thereby a much needed teacher, forester, or medical doctor, the critical middle level manpower shortage remains largely untouched.

In 1964, the Swedish Government sponsored a vocational school at Nimba. Special training programs financed by the United Nations or the United States have made it possible to fill positions such as data processing clerks with Liberians. Nevertheless, vocational education remains one of the most neglected areas in the Liberian education system, despite the critical shortage of workers with this type of training.

Until very recently, higher education received only a nominal amount of foreign assistance; and that which was received generally took the form of teachers and scholarships. In 1962, USAID contracted with Cornell University, under an AID contract, to furnish the University of Liberia with a team of specialists who have worked in the areas of administration, curriculum building and faculty development. Despite the many advances made with

the help of this group in all three areas, there remains much
to be done before the University will equal those in either
Ghana or Nigeria.

Agriculture

Three fundamental objectives have characterized the Liberia
agricultural development program during the period under
review. The first is the long-run objective of achieving self-
sufficiency in the supply of basic foods, especially rice. The
second goal is to expand the opportunities for farmers to
increase their money income. The third objective is to improve
as rapidly as possible the quantity and quality of food consumption. The first two of these objectives are potentially
imcompatible, and experience in Liberia has revealed that this
is actually the case. Maximization of real income is achieved
by employing resources in uses in which their comparative
advantage is greatest. Such an allocation may be consistent with
self-sufficiency in basic foods, but if not, it is necessary to
choose between the conflicting goals. The desire to include
self-sufficiency in the nation's welfare function is understandable, but part of the price of attaining this end is a gap between
the possible and attained real income level; a gap generated by a
less than optimum allocation of resources. The larger the
shortfall of realized income in terms of the optimum level, the
more costly is a policy of self-sufficiency. Liberian climate
and soils favor tree crops compared to food products, and the
highest incomes from agriculture are earned by rubber, coffee,
and cocoa producers. Even more striking is the income differential between farming and mining and service industry employment. Available evidence indicates that migration from
villages of young men has been extremely heavy in recent years,
with the lure of higher incomes being one factor causing this
movement. Since alternate employers favor the brighter, more
energetic, and more educated people, the villages have been
disproportionately depleted of the workers who would best
respond to improved agriculture methods. While this condition
alone need not cause an agricultural program to fail to attain
its objectives, the labor drain from rural areas has caused
extension work to be relatively unproductive in many instances.
Foreign aid to the agriculture sector has been supplied by
FAO, China, Israel and the United States. It has centered

upon research and experimentation, demonstration and training, and forestry development.

The agricultural research program has been centered in the Central Research Station at Suakoko. United States technical personnel assisted the Department of Agriculture and Commerce in this program until about 1962, when AID support was phased out. Since then, the Government has continued to operate the station with the aid of foreign nationals, but the scale and level of operations have been greatly reduced from their former level. The stated reason for the United States withdrawal from this project was that a large body of usable information had been accumulated, the implementation of which would require many years of extension activity. For the time being, it was felt that funds could be more productively utilized elsewhere.

Agriculture demonstration and extension programs have focused upon the training of Liberian extension workers, field trials of new or improved strain crops and production methods, and visits to villages to explain the new techniques and products. During the mid-1950's, the major demonstration work concentrated on swamp rice in the Gbedin Swamp. While high experimental yields were realized, and while some farmers were induced to use the method in practice, the United States gradually lost interest in the project and virtually withdrew its support. The Liberian government, however, remained fascinated by the potentially high rice yields attainable by this method of production. It therefore reactivated the program with the assistance of Chinese technicians in 1962. The new Gbedin program is much more elaborate than the former one. It is a major land resettlement and community development project. As was stated in Chapter 1, this project is extremely capital intensive; this fact, along with the high absolute cost, is causing the Gbedin project to receive all discretionary funds of the Department of Agriculture budget. The success of this program is admittedly very uncertain. Even if it does make a major inroad into the size of the food deficit, such an advantageous outcome will be at the expense of other agriculture programs which are suffering budget curtailments because of it. A sharp cut-back in 1964 of the agriculture extension program is a case in point.

In contrast to the Department of Agriculture approach to demonstration embodied in the Gbedin project are the

demonstration programs of the National Production Council
and private businesses. By coupling demonstration with
processing facilities, such as the Voinjama coffee mill or
Firestone rubber processing facilities, these organizations
have relieved the producer of one of the severe barriers to
increased production. Nevertheless, such factors as
language barriers, the low educational level of typical village
farmers, and both tribal and western land tenure systems
make life difficult for the extension workers. Because it is
believed that extension work will be an unproductive use of
funds until the economic, social and legal barriers to
increased agricultural production are removed, the United
States is withdrawing from this activity. FAO technicians
and the Chinese at Gbedin remain active, but the demonstration and extension phase of agricultural development is presently in a depressed state.

The forestry development phase of agricultural assistance
is about to yield a high pay-off. American foresters have
been working in Liberia since 1951, during which time a
National Forest Reserve plan was implemented, surveys of
forest resources were conducted, and a number of concession
arrangement with private firms were signed. Germany has
provided twelve foresters to assist in forest surveys, and the
United Kingdom and the FAO have both supplied foresters to
teach in the University of Liberia. The Government, under-
standably, is anxious to exploit this resource to its fullest
potential, but a real danger lies in a tendency for the Government to grant overly-liberal concessions in its haste to promote immediate utilization of this natural resource. Harvesting timber on a perpetual yield basis requires extensive
policing of the concession because of the economic inducement
to cut trees at a faster rate than they mature. The small
number of trained Liberian foresters seriously limits the
amount of policing which can be provided at this time. There
exists, therefore, a threat to the continued supply of this
resource if concessions are granted at a rate which exceeds
the availability of supervisory personnel.

Public Administration

Developing and administering a productive technical assistance program in government operations is probably the most

difficult of all forms of external assistance for both donor
and receiver. The difficulty lies in the intimate relationship
which exists between administrative organizations and the
political decision-making process of a country. The dividing
line between recommending a more efficient organization to
the host government and advising it on a basic political
decision is an extremely fine one at best and often it cannot
be perceived. The public administration advisor must constantly choose between two approaches to his work. He may
serve as a pure technician and devise administration systems
to implement the independently determined policies of the
host government. In the case of a policy regarded as undesirable to his government, he is in the anomalous position of
assisting the host country to do better something of which the
donor country disapproves. As an alternative, he can inject
himself into the decision making process, thereby running the
risk of being declared persona non grata by the host country
if he espouses a policy not acceptable to it. The administrative specialist fully realizes that policy making and policy
execution are inseparable components of a whole. The nature
of the policy determines the organization structure required
to optimize its implementation, while at the same time,
administrative weakness can seriously impair the selection of
the best policy; e. g.,not supplying those responsible for
policy decisions with adequate or accurate information.
Coupled with these dilemmas are diplomatic relationships
which must be maintained, often in a state of delicate balance.
Finally, in a small country such as Liberia, the distance
between the chief executive on the one hand and the administrative officers and their advisors on the other is exceedingly
small, so that, willingly or otherwise, the advisor becomes
privy to most policy deliberations. While all technical
advisors must sometimes face this threat from two sides, the
public administration specialist is particularly vulnerable to
it.

It is understandable, therefore, why public administration
activity in sovereign countries such as Liberia has received
less support than other sectors. Until recently, the public
administration function in Liberia was performed solely by
advisors under the name of education or public health assistance.
Some intra-departmental reorganization was accomplished
under the direction of such foreign advisors and even functional

realignments between departments were occasionally
achieved. But these specialists were technical experts, e. g. ,
educators or medical doctors, and organization was not
their main forte. Administrative changes which did occur
were proposed and implemented on an ad hoc basis with the
personal relationship between the department secretary and
the advisor, and between them and the President, often
determining the final outcome. When a change threatened a
second or third echelon administrator, the interplay of
personalities became all-powerful in determining the form
of the final solution.

In 1961, President Tubman requested from the United
States assistance in reorganizing the Liberian government,
including improvement of the budget procedure and introduction of a national planning agency. For decades, Liberia
has maintained a position of leadership in Africa by virtue of
its being one of the two independent tropical African nations.
But with the emergence of thirty or more newly-independent
African states, many with an inherited infrastructure and
trained civil service cadre far superior to those of Liberia,
the country could no longer rely on the independence theme
to guarantee it a voice in African affairs. Economic and
social progress became the accepted test of power on the continent, and Liberia's economy and society proved to be weak
and backward compared to those of others who were bidding
for leadership. Thus, the Liberian leadership perceived that
unless it pursued vigorously a program of economic growth
and social change, its position in Africa would be only nominal. In fact, events already had thrust such new countries
as Ghana into the forefront of African politics, with Liberia
being eclipsed by these newly independent nations.

The public administration program which emerged from
these negotiations with the United States was a commitment
to assist the Liberian Special Commission on Government
Operations (SCOGO) and of aid in establishing a national
economic planning institution. SCOGO has operated in the
tradition of the Hoover Commission in the United States. Each
operating department has been studied, and a reorganization
plan has been prepared for it. These proposals are admittedly
ambitious and full implementation of them will take years due
to a shortage of pro perly trained personnel. Nevertheless,
some progress toward an improved organizational structure
has been realized. The budget procedure has been modernized

and the tax collection administration has been strengthened.
The latter improvement already is yielding positive returns
in the form of increased revenue collections.

Emphasis has been placed on rural government administration; the RAD program at Gbarnga is the pilot project in rural
government. As of June, 1963, slightly more than $2 million
had been committed to this project by AID. The purpose of the
program is to build a strong local government system which
possesses some degree of both fiscal autonomy and control
over the supply of basic services. Many problems have beset
the RAD project. The most serious one stems from the inter-
departmental approach to the supply of technicians and funds.
No two central government departments give the RAD region
the same level of priority in the total department program.
Hence, coordination of individual department efforts has been
difficult. Furthermore, operating departments are not willing
to yield control over their limited resources to a separate (and
new) administrative body.

Other activities of note in the area of government administration and planning are the Census of 1962 conducted with U. S.
technical and financial assistance, the industrial promotion
activities of the Liberia Development Corporation aided by a
United States supported contract team, financial advice from the
International Monetary Fund, the Monrovia City Planning Study
financed by the Federal Republic of Germany, and technical
assistance in planning and statistics supplied by the United
Nations.

Infrastructure Investment

Investment in physical infrastructure facilities has been
late in coming to Liberia in contrast to other African countries,
particularly to those which were formerly under British or
French rule. The first investment of significance was the
Free Port of Monrovia. This was followed in the 1950's by
road construction financed by two Export-Inport Bank loans
totaling $21. 3 million, and the construction of a water and
sewage system in Monrovia aided by a $1. 35 million Export-
Import Bank loan. Two loans from the same source totaling
$12. 02 million financed the expansion of diesel electric power
facilities in 1959 and 1961. Other construction during the late
1950's and early 1960's was financed by government borrowing

from private sources, the first major loans of this sort
negotiated since 1926.

Accompanying most of these loans were surveys and feasibility studies, many financed by external aid. The most
extensive study of this sort was the feasibility analysis of the
Mount Coffee Hydro project, on the basis of which the
Development Loan Fund extended a $24. 3 million credit.
When this project is completed, 30, 000 kw of electrical
power will be added to the existing electric supply in the Monrovia area. Comprehensive studies of the Monrovia water
and sewage system, financed by WHO, have led to DLF
financing of these projects.

Other foreign assistance activities in the area of infrastructure development include a general transportation study
(United States), a series of surveys and studies of the Free
Port (United States), the services of a shipping and port
advisor (Federal Republic of Germany), the construction of
farm-to-market roads in the interior (United States), civil
aviation technicians (International Civil Aviation Organization),
and the training of aviation personnel (Federal Republic of
Germany and Lufthansa).

EFFECTS OF EXTERNAL ASSISTANCE

In spite of the length of the foregoing description of foreign
aid to Liberia, it has not been possible to describe every program or project which was in process at one time or another.
Nevertheless, some inferences may be drawn and conclusions
ventured on the basis of the evidence presented here.

First, the principal supplier of external aid to Liberia has
been and undoubtedly will remain to be, the United States. In
this capacity, the U. S. has exerted a powerful influence on the
character and form of all external aid, since other suppliers
have followed the pattern set by Liberian-United States
cooperation. In many respects, Liberian institutions are
being remodeled in the American image, a development which
imparts a degree of consistency to these changes, but which
also leads to many failures and frustrations because of fundamental differences between the two societies. Some modification of techniques to fit Liberian conditions has occurred.

The further one moves from Monrovia, geographically and

culturally, the more one finds a foreign technician relating himself to indigenous conditions and exhibiting a flexibility toward a particular problem and its solution; an adaptation which is not nearly so evident in the upper strata of technical aid. Nevertheless, the failure to appropriately adapt to local conditions has caused many projects to achieve sub-optimum results. Even technicians from other underdeveloped countries supplied by the United Nations have been guilty at times of the same failure. Liberia, as every other country in the world, is unique. No technology can be transplanted from one country to another without modifications. United States aid officials are becoming aware of the problems which stem from their country's dominance of Liberian external aid. Since 1962, there has been an effort by the United States to separate itself from aid administration, even though it may continue to finance all or most of a project. The increased use of contract rather than direct-hire personnel is one result of this awareness; the channeling of funds through U. N. agencies is another.

Second, foreign aid has not, nor does it claim to have, attacked every existing barrier to economic development. For one reason, neither the full range of such restraints nor their interrelationship is fully understood. For another, some factors known to be critical to the development process are unassailable by economic aid. Foreign economic assistance can help build institutions conducive to progress, it can provide skills and techniques, and it can finance physical capital formation. It cannot, except in the most indirect way, alter attitudes, preconceptions, and beliefs, or develop "initiative, " --the willingness to assume risk. Nor is foreign aid capable of altering the physical conditions of a country or augmenting its natural resource endowments. Foreign aid (and private investment) is able to bring modern technology to bear upon the existing resources to temporarily compensate for a skilled labor shortage, and to supplement the domestic capital supply. But external assistance must always remain a secondary and auxiliary source of factor supplies. Furthermore, foreign aid may render invaluable assistance in the defining of alternative paths of development. At times, it may serve as the catalyst which brings plans and goals to fruition. But foreign technicians can neither define the goals nor make the final selection between alternative development strategies.

Third, correlative to the previous point is the observation

that only by pure chance can aid which is extended and received on an <u>ad</u> <u>hoc</u> basis contain the formula necessary to propel a nation along a self-sustaining growth path. Project oriented aid will, more often than not, be directed toward the squeakiest wheels rather than in the direction of projects and programs possessing the maximum leverage effect. A national plan, formulated on the basis of reliable data and a reasonably defined strategy distilled from analysis of economic and non-economic, national and international factors, is far superior to a shopping list as a framework within which to design and execute specific projects.

Finally, it is possible to venture a few highly tentative generalizations concerning the condition which will determine the degree of success realized by specific foreign aid projects. If foreign aid projects in Liberia were ranked according to how close they come to attaining their original purpose, there emerges a set of conditions which explains why some were notable successes while others fell considerably short of achieving their objectives.

Projects which experience a high degree of success possess at least one, and usually more than one, of the following characteristics: (1) the project centers about skills which are relatively easy to transfer, either because the techniques themselves are simple or because the necessary educated manpower to absorb them was available; (2) the project, administratively, is some distance from a major policy making center; (3) the project has a clearly defined and finite objective; (4) the project has received strong and enthusiastic support from the Liberian Government.

Conversely, the projects which exhibited the largest divergence between realizations and objectives failed to possess most, or all, of these properties apparently necessary for success.

FOOTNOTES

1. For instance, see Truman, "Message to the Congress on Technical Assistance for the Underdeveloped Areas of the World," (Washington: Government Printing Office, June 24, 1949); and D. D. Eisenhower, "Message on Foreign Economic Policy," in United States Senate, Committee on Foreign

Relations, Development of Technical Assistance Programs
(Washington: Government Printing Office, 1954).

2. "Illogical, Shutting Down Roberts Field," Time,
May 12, 1947, pp. 37-28.

3. M. Curti and K. Birr, Prelude to Point Four (Madison:
University of Wisconsin Press, 1954), p. 70. Harvey Firestone agreed to consider building a port in 1926, but the project was dropped when it was found to be much more expensive than had been anticipated. J. C. Young, Liberia
Rediscovered (Garden City: Doubleday, Doran and Company,
1934), p. 36.

4. The practical reason was that the Navy Department could
not spare manpower at that time. The legal reason was that
the Republic of Liberia was technically the builder and by
the time construction began, the port had been redesigned as
a commercial installation with the United States having only
a contingency right to use it for military purposes.

5. J. F. Sly, and W. P. Heddon, The Free Port and Harbor
of Monrovia, Republic of Liberia (Washington: Department
of State, March 1, 1954).

6. Export-Import Bank of Washington, Fourteenth Semi-
Annual Report to Congress, January-June, 1952 (Washington:
Government Printing Office, 1952), pp. 58-59; United States
Department of Commerce, Foreign Aid of the United States
Government (Washington: Government Printing Office,
p. 99.

7. E. P. Hanson, "Missionaries and Foreign Economic
Administration," address by Dr. Hanson, Special representative, Foreign Economic Administration, (Monrovia, July 19,
1945).

8. See M. B. Shimkin, Report on the United States Public
Health Service Mission in Liberia, May 3-25, 1946 (Washington: Office of International Health Relations, 1945), passim.

9. Mayer, op, cit.

10. "Mission to Liberia, " Scientific American, 179 (December, 1948), p. 27.

11. Foreign Economic Administration, Summary Progress Report of Technical Activities. For reasons best known to the responsible persons, this phase of technical assistance was not made part of the Point Four Mission after 1951. Not until 1957 was sufficient interest in small business sufficiently strong to warrant an American specialist being attached to the Mission in Liberia.

12. W. V. S. Tubman, First Annual Message, (Monrovia: 1944), p. 30.

13. While the Economic and Public Health Missions were pursuing studies leading to the assembling of such information, their work had progressed little beyond the initial explanatory stage by 1946. The significance is that no mention of the existing body of knowledge of resources appeared in the Plan.

14. Testimony of Under Secretary of State, James Webb, in United States Congress, International Technical Cooperation Act of 1949 Hearings, Part I, p. 7.

15. W. V. S. Tubman, First Annual Message, (Monrovia:1952).

16. The first step taken by the Planning Agency was to initiate an effective and continuous flow of facts about the economy, without which intelligent decisions could not be made. The most intensive statistical exercise was the 1962 Census and the most extensive study was the Economic Survey of Liberia carried out with the assistance of a team from Northwestern University. A team under a USAID contract with Klein & Saks, Inc. , a private United States management consulting firm, undertook to establish the Office of National Planning as an operating entity, including the training of program planning officers and ONP personnel. Presently a group from Harvard University is engaged in the actual formulation of a development plan.

17. For a complete description of fundamental education, see Department of Public Instruction, Fourth Annual Report, 1955.

CHAPTER 7 HISTORY AND THE FUTURE

The impact upon an underdeveloped economy of an inflow of foreign public and private investment and technical assistance is multi-valued. Such factors as the structure of the industry, the legal form of the investment, the economic and political motivations of the investor, and the political and social climate vis-a-vis foreign investment in the host country are but a few of the many determinants of the form and magnitude of the economic consequences of foreign investment in an underdeveloped country. The impact itself also exhibits numerous facets. Quantitative measures such as production, employment, income, consumption, domestic saving and investment, and population changes present a significant albeit a partial, picture of the changes wrought upon an underdeveloped economy by foreign investment and trade. In addition, capital imports generate contacts between two or more significantly different cultures from which changes in customs, habits, behavior and institutions almost invariably emerge. While all parties involved in the process of international investment are affected by these cultural confrontations, it is the people of the host country who experience the most dramatic alteration of their previous way of life since their country serves as the meeting ground of the domestic and alien cultural systems. The conflicting tugs of traditional culture on the one hand, and the fascination of modern technology and attraction of rising real incomes on the other have caused all facets of Liberian society to be afflicted with frustrations and conflicts caused by these two antagonistic pulls. It has not been possible in this study to effectively deal with these aspects of economic development. The interested reader is referred to works by such writers as Melville Herskovits, Marion Levy, Margaret Mead, Warren D'Azivido and Dr. George W. Harley, who, as trained anthropologists, have produced excellent studies on the impact of modern technology and culture upon a pre-machine tribal society.

LIBERIA IN 1940

The Liberian economy of 1940 may best be described as a
stationary state. A large subsistence sector embraced no
less than 90 per cent of the total population. Almost all output was produced with traditional and inefficient methods. Per
capita income was extremely low, and few indigenous products
entered into the money economy. Economic, social, and
political contacts between the rural people and the Americo-
Liberians who occupied the littoral areas were few. The lack
of roads and communication facilities, in addition to a cultural
hiatus between these population groups, were the principal
causes of there being "two Liberias."

Standing somewhat apart from the domestic economy was
the Liberian rubber industry. While dominated by the Firestone Plantations Company, the industry did include a handful
of Liberian producers. Most of the latter firms were modest
plantations, owned in the main by "honorables" or by members
of Liberia's "first families." In 1940, rubber accounted for
70 per cent of all exports. Raw gold was the only other export
of consequence, accounting for 10 per cent of the total. Virtually all of the remainder was in cocoa, coffee, palm kernels,
oils, and piassava. Total exports in 1940 amounted to $3.2
million while imports aggregated $1.9 million. The amount of
capital inflow in that year was probably small. The remainder
of the balance of payments consisted of Liberian purchases of
services abroad, outflow of earnings on foreign investments in
Liberia, and an outflow of private Liberian capital. Major
imports were petroleum products, machinery and motor
vehicles, food, and beverages. A large share of these products
were destined for sale to Firestone, other foreign concessionaires, and a few well-to-do citizens rather than the general
population. [1]

The rate of internal investment in Liberia in 1940 is reputed
to be very low. The only domestic capital formation known for
certain was by the government. Total revenues amounted to
only $750,000 in that year, against which the government
spent $636,000 for current operating expenditures. [2] The
principal revenue sources were the hut tax which yielded $268,-
000 and customs revenues which accounted for $431,000. Expen-
ditures for capital development at this time were practically

nil. Total outlays for education, public health, transportation and public enterprises were, in 1943, $34,000, $51,000, $57,000, and $87,000 respectively. Outlays for the same purposes in 1940 were no larger, and possibly were less than these amounts. No more than 10 per cent of these amounts was allocated to new capital formation. [3]

Accounting for a very low rate of domestic capital formation in 1940 were such factors as low per capita income, an extremely unequal distribution of income, a preference by those who could save for hoarding or speculation in real estate, no financial system into which savings could be channeled for productive use, and a government which maintained, at best, only nominal control over the interior and which inspired little confidence in the majority of the population. In addition to these economic and institutional factors which impeded capital formation, there was an illiteracy rate in excess of 90 per cent, and generally poor conditions of health and diet on the part of almost everyone in Liberia.

EXTERNAL ECONOMIC SHOCKS

The most dramatic shock to the Liberian economy during the 1940-1950 decade was the construction of the Free Port of Monrovia, which was an outgrowth of the utilization of Liberia's strategic location on the west coast of Africa by the Allied Powers during World War II. In addition the United States Army built several miles of roads and constructed Roberts Field. At the close of the War an Economic Mission and a Public Health Mission were dispatched to Liberia by the United States Government. General world economic conditions during the immediate post-war years also reacted to Liberia's benefit. During World War II and again during the Korean War, rubber prices rose sharply, generating not only immediate increases in personal and government incomes, but stimulating also further Liberian and foreign investment in rubber production. The known existence of exceptionally rich iron ore deposits, the search by American producers for additional raw material supplies, and the modern port all combined to bring forth the investment by the Liberia Mining Company at Bomi Hills. In addition, a spontaneous growth of interest in Liberia developed on the part of some other foreign business firms after the close of World War II. In part, this interest was the result of a growing market within Liberia for consumer and capital goods. Of greater importance, however, in explaining private and public American interest in the West African Republic were such developments as (1) the world-wide concern over the economic development of underdeveloped countries, (2) the emerging political nationalism among African countries in general, (3) increased knowledge of African natural resources and peoples, and (4) the technological developments since 1940 which made travel to and life in tropical Africa at least tolerable for Americans and Europeans. Finally, the post-war European dollar shortage stimulated a movement of private European business enterprises into Liberia because of its convertible dollar currency.

The enunciation of the Point Four concept by President Truman in 1949 led to a formalization of United States technical and capital assistance to Liberia, which continues to dominate the total inflow of foreign assistance from foreign governments and international bodies.

Beginning in 1955, a second wave of foreign investment inundated the country. Rubber, other tree crop producers, and mining firms negotiated for and received concessions. The Liberia-American Minerals Company is the largest single investment in Liberia. In its first full year of operation this company's production was equal to the previous total output of iron ore.

The entire flow of foreign investment into Liberia during the period 1940-1963 has been phenomenal. Foreign private investment amounted to no less than $420 million. United States development loans extended both to the government and to private industry amounted to $76 million during the same period. In addition, the Liberian government borrowed some $86 million in foreign capital markets. Thus, the total capital investment financed from abroad equaled at least $581 million, and a probably larger total would emerge if loans by commercial and banking enterprises were included. In addition, United States grant assistance for the period exceeded $40 million to which contributions by the United Nations and by other countries must be added. From these summary totals, an annual rate of foreign capital and technical assistance inflow of $27 million is calculated. These investment, coupled with Liberian government expenditures for development financed from current revenues, themselves largely a product of the operation of foreign enterprises, account for virtually all of the capital formation in Liberia since 1940.

PRIMARY ECONOMIC EFFECTS

In order to portray the variety of economic effects induced by foreign public and private investment upon an underdeveloped economy, a two-fold classification of the consequences will be employed. <u>Primary effects</u> are those relating to the making of the investment as well as to its subsequent operation. Measures of these primary effects are employment and income generated by foreign business and Liberian Government programs, food and other production directly generated by technical assistance programs, and exports of merchandise. <u>Secondary effects</u> relate to those economic consequences of foreign investment which are induced by, but are operationally independent of, the primary investment. Specific measures of secondary effects are government receipts and public expenditures, Liberian consumption expenditures, and domestic private investment.

Employment and Income

In 1940, the number of Liberians employed in the money sector probably did not exceed 20,000, of which 18,000 were working for Firestone. With a labor force size of 150,000 at that time, the money sector participation rate was about 13 per cent. Beginning in 1944, wage employment rose to an estimated 40,000, of which 23,000 were employed by Firestone.[4] By 1955, total employment reached 55,000 and by 1964 it had attained a level of 90,000. In this last year, a money sector labor participation rate of almost 35 per cent is calculated based upon an estimated labor force of 260,000.

The only year for which careful estimates of national income have been made are for 1960, when the level of Gross Domestic Money Income stood at $154 million. Estimates for 1950 place the level of total incomes at $35.8 million and for 1964 at $180 million. From this data it can be seen that total production and income have been rising at an exceedingly high rate. However, a considerable portion of the income generated by production accrues to foreigners, a high percentage of which is repatriated by the recipients. Wage income earned by Liberians in 1960 is

estimated at $47 million compared with an estimated $3.2
million in 1940 and $8 million in 1955. Real wages have not
risen as rapidly, especially in recent years when annual
price increases of certain basic staples and services of from
10 to as high as 100 per cent have been reported. [5] At the same
time, the money sector labor force has increased 4.5 times
since 1940, while money wage payments have been multiplied
by a factor of 12. Even allowing for price increases, a rise
in real per capita income of at least 100 per cent on the part
of wage employees is noted. Since real wages in the money
sector exceed those in the subsistence sector by a considerable amount, a comparison between money and tribal sector
incomes would show a much larger increase in real income
for those people who have migrated from the villages to urban
areas.

Despite the rapid increase in employment, there remains a
severe labor shortage in Liberia, especially of semi-skilled,
skilled, and professional workers. A considerable portion of
foreign aid and wage incomes generated by foreign concessions
is therefore dissipated in the form of payments to expatriate
personnel whose annual cost is 6 to 10 times that of a Liberian
engaged in the same activity. The supply of physical capital
does not appear to be nearly the bottleneck to economic growth
as does the supply of trained workers. Human resource
development must be given first priority in development planning for several years if labor productivity is to rise.

Food Production

Foreign public investment, including technical assistance,
has had two types of direct effects upon the native Liberian
economy. First, there has been some change in the type of
food produced as a result of United States agricultural technical assistance programs. Second, technical assistance in
education and public health and capital investment in transportation have created the external economies which stimulate
village production for sale in the money economy. Available
data dealing with subsistence agriculture are scanty, and tem-
poral comparisons cannot be easily made of the quantities produced. However, it is the concensus of agricultural technicians
and others close to agriculture that total food, and particularly
rice, production has declined, at least since 1951 despite
increases in some areas.

One index of food production in Liberia is the behavior of food imports. Imports of foodstuffs increased from $10 million to $15 million between 1961 and 1963. Rice imports amounted to 39,000 metric tons in 1963 compared to 8,600 metric tons in 1955. The principal reason advanced to explain a diminution in subsistance agriculture is that labor has been drawn away from the villages by competing economic opportunities. As a corollary to this direct cause of lowered food production is the disintegration of tribal society caused by economic change in Liberia. As the tribal society has become disorganized, agricultural production has suffered.

While alternative economic opportunities and social change brought about by the infusion of foreign investment into Liberia are convenient reasons for explaining the apparent failure of technical assistance programs to raise agricultural output, there is another cause of this phenomenon. Agricultural technical assistance rendered by the United States and the United Nations has been devoted largely to surveys, basic research and experiments with new and varied crop and animal strains. The surveys pointed up many of the shortcomings and needs of the Liberian farmer, basic research isolated several causes of production problems, and experimentation indicated which types and strains of crops and animals were amenable to Liberian conditions. But, despite the enormous amount of knowledge so gained, the impact upon the bush farmer in the form of food either to eat or to sell was small.

Viewed in terms of realized production to date, the technical assistance program in agricultural extension has been only slightly successful. Agricultural extension is an inherently slow activity because of the time required both to learn new techniques, and unlearn old ones, and to acquire the necessary complementary factors of production. Farmers in general, and Liberian farmers in particular, have a very pragmatic view of agricultural technology. They have learned through trial and error what will and will not work. Living as close as they do to a subsistence level, Liberian farmers must be convinced that a new method has a high probability of success before they will risk abandonment of a known and proven technology for a new one. While the low educational level of typical tribal farmers is a handicap to gaining acceptance of new methods and crops, the proven success of a new technique remains the best teacher. On the other hand, the farmer, no matter how

desirous he may be to increase his production, will gain very
little unless the agricultural extension workers themselves are
well trained and able to transmit their knowledge to the farmer.
Few extension workers appreciate the problems of the village
farmer and fewer still lack the experience necessary to adapt
new techniques to local conditions. The creation of a skill
and attitude base conducive to further learning is the first job
of any teacher, especially when he operates in a culture in
which risk taking and change are alien qualities. Often a
generation must pass before the psychological and informational infrastructure required for expanded agricultural production is created. Impatience with this time consuming phase
of learning has led to the institution of a number of highly publicized crash programs at the expense of basic education. Some
have criticized AID for withdrawing from agricultural extension activity in favor of rural education projects. However,
this policy is culturally sound as it recognizes that basic skill
development is a prerequisite for successful informational
exchange programs.

Exports

The importance of foreign trade to the Liberian economy is
indicated by the ratio of trade to national income. In 1960,
exports were almost 54 per cent of Gross Domestic Money
Income, and imports were 45 per cent of the same total. This
high dependence on trade places the economy at the mercy of
fluctuations of world prices of rubber and iron ore, and to a
lesser extent, of those of coffee, cocoa, and palm kernels.
Virtually all foreign concessions produce for export and a pre-
dominance of Liberian enterprises are likewise oriented.
Within the economy, the export industries exhibit a higher
level of productivity than do those producing for domestic sale
or subsistence consumption.

The relation between exports and other aggregate indices of
economic performance are summarized in Figure I. Between
1940 and 1950, the correlation between the expansion of exports
and revenue is readily apparent. In 1950 and 1951, exports
rose sharply reflecting the impact of the Korean War on rubber
prices. Revenues likewise exhibited a phenomenal increase,
tripling between 1950 and 1951. In addition to the increase in
rubber prices, a further cause of this sharp rise was the first

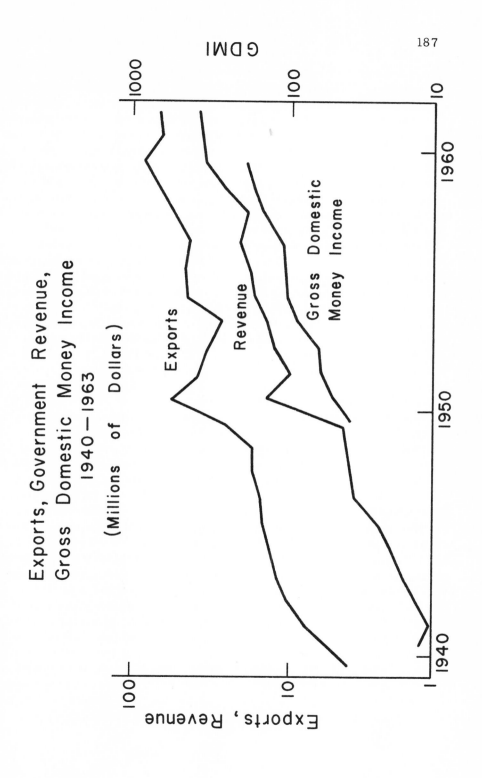

Exports, Government Revenue,
Gross Domestic Money Income
1940–1963

(Millions of Dollars)

payment by Firestone of income tax under the Income Tax
Law of 1950. Between 1951 and 1954, revenues continued to
expand as a consequence of new taxes and of the emergence of
additional sources of revenue, both of which off-set the negative effect of falling rubber prices during this period. Between
1954 and 1963, revenues and exports experienced parallel
growth rates. Revenues exhibited the same cyclical pattern
as exports but with a lag of one year. Gross Domestic Money
Income expanded at about the same rate as the other two series
and with the same cyclical pattern as exports, but with much
more dampened fluctuations.

Another little noted effect of foreign trade is its control
over the quantity of money in circulation. Exports and capital
inflows lead to an expansion of the money supply; imports and
capital outflow, including repatriated earnings of foreign firms,
cause it to contract. Given the high ratio of trade to total
economic activity, the high marginal propensity to import by
both Liberians and foreigners, and the almost exclusive control
of trade by foreign business firms, the importance of the trade
balance-money supply relationship to the economy is apparent.
Since both export and import prices are externally determined,
the principal impact of a shift in the trade and
capital account balance is on incomes rather than the price
level.

The total value of exports and imports is given in Table 13.
Two significant conclusions may be drawn from an examination
of export data. The first is that a rapid expansion of both
volume and value has occurred between 1940 and 1963, especially
during the War years of 1940-1944 and again in 1950-1951. The
second feature of total exports is the fact that they have been
subjected to wider cyclical fluctuations than have imports. The
slow increase in import volume during the World War II period
followed by the sharp resurgence recorded for the years 1945-
1947 is explained by the war-caused shipping shortage which
led to an artificially depressed import level during the war.
Before 1950, the level was almost exclusively determined by
export volume. After this date, a growing share of imports
was devoted to capital formation, the demand for which is
more independent of current income than is the demand for
imports for consumption.

By commodity group, total exports are dominated by rubber

and iron ore.   Rubber exports totaled $25. 7 million in 1962, and iron ore amounted to $32. 4 million.   The combined total of these two commodities accounted for 86 per cent of 1962 exports.   In 1963, these two products comprised 88 per cent of total exports, and in 1955 they were 94 per cent of the total.

Other export products contribute only slightly to the national income.   Only diamonds are of any significance at present, the total value in 1962 amounting to $4. 6 million or 6. 8 per cent of total exports.   Palm kernels, once a significant crop, have fallen in value in recent years principally because of reduced output due to labor migration to urban areas.

Thus, the Liberian economy remains dominated by two commodities.   Furthermore, between 65 and 70 per cent of all exports are produced by foreign firms, causing capital flows and repatriated earnings to bulk large in the balance of payments and to control incomes and the money supply.

SECONDARY EFFECTS

Some years ago, H. W. Singer presented an analysis of the impact of foreign investment on a developing economy, and concluded that most of the multiplier-accelerator and external economy effects of foreign investment accrued to the industrial economy supplying the capital rather than to the host country. [6] However, he modifies this position somewhat in a footnote reference to the capacity of the government of an underdeveloped country to capture gains for itself through tax and royalty payments by foreign-owned businesses.   The chance to use income from foreign investment, Singer asserts, is "a chance more often missed than caught by the fore-lock. " [7] The history of Liberian fiscal operations between 1940 and 1963 indicates what the effects on the rate of economic development may be when foreign-owned income is caught and used.

Converting income of foreign operations into concrete projects, and into meaningful economic gains for the society, involves two steps.   The income must first be acquired by the government through taxes, royalties, profit sharing or fees. Secondly, judicious use of such funds must be made by the authorities.   One inherent danger of a rapid rise in government income is that inefficiencies in its use are almost bound to occur.

When Liberian government revenue tripled between 1950 and
1951, expenditures were expanded in almost every direction.
Inadequate advance planning of how to use these receipts
resulted in projects being undertaken which often represented
ineffective and, at times, a complete waste of resources. In
1959-1963, based on the expectation of iron ore royalties, a
large increase in government expenditures took place with
somewhat the same result.

Public policy may also control and direct the distribution of
gains from foreign investment in other ways. Such devices as
requirements that a minimum amount of capital invested by
foreign entrepreneurs be supplied by citizens, that control in
whole or in part be exercised by the government or by citizens
of the host country, or that a minimum number of employees
and supervisors be citizens of the underdeveloped country are
methods whereby additional benefits of the investment may be
gained. Control over the use of personal income earned by
residents of the host country is possible by import levies to
reduce consumption spending either in the aggregate or for
particular commodities. Complementary measures to increase
domestic saving and promote investment may also be employed,
although Liberia so far has not done as much in this area as
she could.

Public Revenues

In 1940, Liberian government revenues totaled $800,000 with
customs receipts providing the major part of the total. By
1950, revenues had risen to $3.9 million with essentially the
same fiscal tax structure as in 1940.

It was in 1951 that the most dramatic change in revenues
directly attributable to foreign investment and economic
development took place. In that year, the first payment by
Firestone added more than $7 million to total revenue. In 1953,
iron ore mining royalties began to be received, adding $2 mil-
lion per year to government income. Also, after 1950, new
levies such as the General Sales Tax began to produce rapidly
increasing yields which reflected the expansion of the money
economy of the country. New levies were added to the fiscal
structure, such as a Luxury Tax in 1951 and a Health Tax in
1953. Customs revenues, while expanding in absolute terms,
underwent a relative decline in the face of these new sources of

revenue. In addition to these ordinary forms of taxation, income from shipping registrations began to achieve an important place in the fiscal system. By 1955, this income source yielded $1.1 million or about 7 per cent of total receipts.

By 1960, the budget had risen to $33 million with iron ore royalties and rubber income tax payments providing about 40 per cent of the total. Beginning in that year, a set of budgetary pressures became operative, culminating in the crisis of 1963-1964. Rubber and iron ore prices both began to fall. Rubber, selling at 37 cents per pound in 1960, was bringing only 26 cents in 1963. The price of iron ore fell from $11.90 per ton in 1960 to $7.03 per ton in 1963. While both iron ore and rubber export volume increased in 1961-1963, the expansion was not sufficient to offset these price declines so that the net result was a reduction in government revenue from these two sources.

The second set of forces was the influx of several new concessions which imposed on the government a demand for additional services, and indirectly affected the budget by attracting skilled labor through higher wage rates.

Finally, the government came face to face with the necessity of retiring the $86 million short term debt contracted between 1959 and 1962. Unable to meet the scheduled repayments, Liberia appealed to the International Monetary Fund for, and received, a stand-by agreement and a negotiated reduction of debt-service payments in exchange for the institution of a program of budgetary austerity.

Dependence upon foreign concessions for revenue to finance operating and development activities is a two-edged sword which can cut deeply at times into both the public and private sectors of the economy. Not only are government projects retrenched or halted when exports fall, but new private investment is inhibited during periods of stress. Planning and execution of development programs become difficult, and the inflow of foreign capital investment is adversely affected.

Personal Money Income and Its Use

Although detailed studies of personal consumption expenditures for Liberia are not available, imports offer some indication of the use of personal income. Of total imports of $107 million in 1963, almost $20 million consisted of food, beverages, and tobacco products (see Table 23). It is estimated that $16.5 million of this total was sold to Liberians. Another $20 million, mostly manufactured goods, may be considered to have been consumed. Using a total of $36.5 million of imports for consumption by Liberians, an average propensity to import of 10.5 per cent is calculated against Gross Domestic Money Income, and about 40 per cent against Liberian personal income plus government revenue. While these measures of the average propensity to import are crudely compounded from a series of estimates, they imply a high propensity to purchase imported goods.

The implications of a high propensity to import are several. The expenditure of money income from foreign investment and trade on imports does not provide a major stimulus to the rest of the economy to invest and produce goods. Moreover, importing is largely done by foreign firms so that income from merchandising accrues to non-Liberians. Finally, because imports occupy the primary position in Liberian consumption, the price level in supplier countries exerts a major effect upon the level of living in Liberia.

Private Liberian Investment

A principal index of the impact of foreign private business in an underdeveloped country is the extent to which it stimulates the domestic country to produce and invest. Singer doubts very much that the secondary multiplier effects of foreign investment upon the domestic country are significant. On the other hand, studies of private foreign business investment, such as those of the National Planning Association, have concluded that, in general, "certain, though not all, United States private enterprises operating in foreign countries have made contributions to the welfare of these countries, and that these contributions have resulted from the foresight of management." [8]

There are three basic ways by which foreign businesses may stimulate the domestic economy of a country. The first is by providing incentives to private domestic investment by direct purchase from local firms or by the extension of external economies to such enterprises. A partial list of such contributions includes:

1. Using natural resources in a more productive fashion.
2. Employing labor at higher incomes than are being earned

in other sectors.

3. Generating local enterprise by purchases of products consumed by the country.

4. Developing a domestic industry producing the same product as the foreign firm.

5. Building roads, power plants and other physical capital assets which exude external economies to domestic producers.

6. Teaching skills which are transferable to other lines of production.

The second principal form of contribution to the local economy is the alteration of economic institutions in a way favorable to private entrepreneurial activity. Some of the important institutions affected by private enterprise are:

1. Standard of business operation, including record keeping and management techniques.

2. Personnel policies, including hiring, training, promotion, workman's compensation, and pension and retirement policies.

3. Finance and banking techniques and institutions.

4. Land tenure systems which may have to be altered to accomodate both the foreign business and the new enterprises which they foster.

5. Education which may be turned toward a functional curriculum and away from one oriented to classical or religious subjects.

Foreign enterprise and public assistance may also influence domestic attitudes in such ways as:

1. Creating a respect for manual work and pride of craftsmanship.

2. Altering consumption habits which creates the desire for furthering economic change.

3. Substituting the idea of success in business for government employment as a road to personal prestige.

4. Changing attitudes toward authority, such as the willingness to accept the discipline of the factory and the authority of a boss who was chosen for his ability instead of his age, birth, or social position.

5. Generating acceptance of the concepts of the sanctity of contract and the corporate form of investment.

6. Developing a willingness to accept risk.

Table 23: Imports by Commodity Class--Liberia, 1955-1963

Commodity Class	1955	1956	1957	1958	1959	1960	1961	1962	1963
All Commodities	26.0	26.8	38.3	38.5	42.9	69.2	90.7	131.6	106.9
Food, Beverages & Tobacco	5.7	5.0	7.2	8.2	7.8	11.0	14.1	17.0	19.7
Machinery & Vehicles	6.4	6.5	11.4	10.4	10.4	23.3	35.0	53.7	31.0
Chemicals	2.1	1.9	2.3	2.7	2.7	4.7	4.3	5.8	4.8
Manufactured Goods	10.0	11.7	15.2	14.3	18.7	26.2	31.5	47.1	40.6
Fuels and Lubricants	1.4	1.3	1.7	2.7	2.8	2.9	3.4	4.3	7.5
Others	0.4	0.4	0.5	0.2	0.5	1.1	2.4	3.7	3.2

Source: Republic of Liberia, Bureau of Statistics, Foreign Trade Supplements, selected years.

This suggested list of possible effects of foreign investment upon the domestic economy is an imposing one, especially if they are all regarded as being positive contributions. Many students of primitive societies, and especially anthropologists, would hasten to charge that the list is loaded with value judgments, and that all of these changes wrought by people from another culture are not necessarily beneficial to the citizens of the underdeveloped country. Foreign capital and technology may lead to higher production, but unless the society wants the types of goods made available, and accepts the altered income distribution which accompanies the new technology, it cannot be said that "welfare" has necessarily been increased. This criticism of foreign public and private investment cannot be ignored in an evaluation of such investment in a pre-machine economy, but it is preferable to view cultural factors as restraints on the rate and form of economic development rather than as immutable barriers which block all change.

Examples of almost every particular category of social and economic change caused by foreign investment may be found in Liberia. Rubber and iron ore concessionaires have turned jungle into productive acreage and have given employment to many thousands of Liberians, both directly and indirectly. These people earn incomes substantially higher than in the subsistence sector, and many have learned new skills which are transferrable to other employment. One firm introduced a Workman's Compensation scheme which has become the legal standard of the country. Local enterprise has been stimulated, the most notable case being the more than 3000 independent rubber producers who were promoted under the aegis of Firestone. Roads built by concessions are open to public use. For their employees, the companies have furnished schools, hospitals and housing.

At the same time, there is some feeling among a few Liberians that private employers have not done all that they could to spark internal development. Foreign firms are charged with failing to train Liberians for supervisory positions, with not actively fostering local production of goods which the firm uses, and with confining their education and health programs to their won employees. How much of this attitude is the result of a case of infectious xenophobia, transmitted from other African nations, is difficult to determine. Some isolated cases can be discovered to support the claims. The counter-charge is that

qualified Liberians do not often seek jobs as supervisors, are
more interested in entering government service than private
business, and that national health and education programs are
the responsibility of the government, which the firms support
through tax and royalty payments.

A number of the alledged causes of why few Liberians are
in private business are those over which foreign investors as
well as United States and United Nations technicians have little
or no direct control. Education, public health, technical
knowledge, transportation, and power facilities are the
ingredients for economic development. But the attitudes
toward new forms of labor, the centralization of political
power in the hands of one party, the communal society of the
tribes, and all of the other economic, institutional, social and
cultural forces which make up Liberia somehow must adapt
themselves to these ingredients. Economic development
means complete social change, whereby all of the social elements must be reordered and rearranged.

PAST AND FUTURE

Several of the social and institutional factors which have
been diagnosed as being causes of underdevelopment are under-
going change in Liberia. The government is bringing its
organizational form more into line with the requirements for a
dynamic development process. The budget process is being
modernized to cope with revenues of $150 million per year. A
national economic planning machinery is slowly being integrated
into the decision-making structure of government. Younger
"honorables," while still occupying high government posts, are
supplementing their income by private business activity, and
some are leaving government service to devote full time to
their personal business. A statement was made to the writer
in 1956 that "Liberians are more interested in selling concessions to others than in undertaking their own investment."
This generalization does not do justice to the many small, and
even some very large, Liberian sponsored and financed business
enterprises which have been established since 1950.

The fact remains, however, that the bulk of income and
production emanates from primary commodity exports, which
means foreign enterprises for the most part. Development
capital financing and technical assistance from abroad continue

to dominate the public sector despite the rapid rise of government revenues in recent years. Without foreign assistance the economy would be operating at a level well below its present scale.

The most critical demands of the Liberian economy at present are for more domestic capital formation and for development of the nation's human resource potential. Domestic investment in both private and public sectors must replace foreign capital and technical assistance as the predominant supply of these resources. The application of presently employed techniques designed to promote domestic investment will have to be intensified, and new tools of economic policy may need to be introduced. An example of this latter category of needs is a proposed plan for a national currency and central bank which should be critically reexamined. These monetary institutions would provide to development planners the fiscal and monetary tools currently in use in other countries but presently absent in Liberia.

Without a large and expanding cadre of trained people, any tendency toward achieving self-sustaining development will be thwarted as it has been in the past. The recent shift by both the Liberian government and foreign aid donors toward education is most welcome, but more than high hopes or even larger expenditures of money is required to close the crucial man-power gap. The present educational program recognizes the enormity of the man-power problem in Liberia, but a clearly specified course of action for solving it is lacking. Resources are spread over too many areas so that no one is receiving the minimum critical effort necessary to set the entire machine into motion. It is suggested that secondary education and vocational training receive first priority until the middle and high level man-power gap is significantly reduced. As this is accomplished, trained people will be able to fill the teaching positions in an expanded elementary school program, meet the demand in industry and government for trained workers, or enter the university for professional education.

Foreign private and public investment and technical assistance have left an indelible mark upon the economy of Liberia, and have provided it with a basic structure from which can emerge an auto-generating process of economic development. The economy has grown, but it has not yet developed in the sense of having attained a state whereby the proceeds of past expansion are capable of carrying the bulk of future expansion.

When this stage of economic development is achieved, foreign investment and aid can be relegated to a marginal position in the process instead of serving as the prime movers.

So long as Liberia must rely primarily on rubber and iron ore exports, the economic future is not optimistic. Rubber prices are not likely to recover from their present level except during an abnormal demand situation such as a major war, and they may well fall further in the future under the pressure of advancing synthetic rubber technology. While the recent decline of iron ore prices may be temporary, the fact remains that this resource is exhaustible and a time will come when profit sharing incomes will cease to expand and then become less. The one bright spot in the picture is the time interval before this adverse reaction becomes a reality. This time element is one of the two most important economic resources available to Liberia today. The other is the desire and ability of the people, and particularly of the new elite , to use it profitably.

FOOTNOTES

1. No detailed balance of payments had been published by the Liberian Government prior to 1953.

2. Steadman, op. cit. , pp. 83-84.

3. Ibid. , Section D.

4. Republic of Liberia, Department of the Treasury, Annual Report of the Financial Advisor, (Monrovia: 1944).

5. Office of National Planning, Annual Report, 1963-1964, pp. 12-13.

6. Singer, op. cit.

7. Ibid. , p. 475, n. 3.

8. Taylor, op. cit. , p. 108. See also American Enterprise Association, American Private Enterprise, Foreign Economic Development, and the Aid Programs, (Washington: Government Printing Office, 1947); a study of private foreign investment.

Principal Agricultural and Timbering Concessions in Liberia, 1960

Company	Date of Agreement (a)	Area Granted (acres)	Duration (years)	Principal Tax Provisions (b)
Firestone Plantations Company	1926	1,000,000	99	Subject to income tax
Liberia Company	1947	150,000	40	12 yr. income tax exemption (now expired) 25% of net profits paid to GOL and 10% to the Liberia Foundation
African Fruit Company	1953	600,000	80	Income tax exemption has expired. Now subject to income tax.
B. F. Goodrich	1954	600,000	80/10 (c)	16.5 yr. income tax exemption and 25% of net income exempt for next 10 years.
R. G. LeTourneau	1954	500,000	80/30 (d)	
Liberia Industrial Forestry Corporation	1957	40,000	20	5 yr. income tax exemption. Rent of 8¢ per acre.

Principal Agricultural and Timbering Concessions in Liberia, 1960 Cont.

Company	Year	Acreage		Terms
Morro River Lumber Company	1957	100,000	60	5 yr. income tax exemption. Rent of 6¢ per acre.
Liberian Agricultural Company	1959	600,000	70	15 yr. income tax exemption and 25% of net income exempt for next 10 years.
Siga Lumber Company	1959	40,000	60	5 yr. income tax exemption. Rent of 6¢ per acre.
Liberia Timber Industries Corporation	1959	450,000	45 and option to add 25	10 yr. income tax exemption. Rent of 10¢ per acre.
Salala Rubber Company	1960	10,000	70	14 yr. income tax exemption.
Maryland Logging Company	1960	500,000	45 and option to add 25	10 yr. income tax exemption. Rent of 10¢ per acre.

Principal Agricultural and Timbering Concessions in
Liberia, 1960 Cont.

(a) Legislative Approval
(b) All concessions may import duty free all supplies and
equipment required for operation of the enterprise.
(c) Eighty years for developed land. Land not developed in
ten years reverts to the Government.
(d) Eighty years for developed land. Land not developed in
thirty years reverts to the Government.
* *

Principal Mining Concessions in Liberia

Company	Date of Agreement	Terms of Agreement	Major Tax Provisions
Liberia Mining Co. (LMC)	1946	30 yrs.	25% of net profits to GOL, 1952-1959 35% of net profits to GOL, 1960-1969 50% of net profits to GOL, thereafter
National Iron Ore Company (NIOC)	1958	80 yrs.	Dividends on 50% of common stock purchased by GOL.
Deutsche-Liberian Mining Co. (DELIMCO)	1958	70 yrs.	50% of net profits to GOL.
LAMCO Joint Venture (Liberian American Swedish Minerals Co. and Bethlehem Steel Corp.	1953/ 1960 (a)	70 yrs.	Bethlehem Steel Corp. pays 50% of its net profit. LAMCO pays 50¢ per ton royalty in 1963-64, and 50% of net profits thereafter.

(a) LAMCO signed the original concession agreement in 1953.
The expanded enterprise, known as the LAMCO Joint Venture
was formed in 1960.

Wage Rates of Unskilled Labor--Selected Countries in
West Africa, 1948 or 1949

City and Country	Daily Wage (local currency)	Daily Wage (U.S. dollars)	Year
Leopoldville, Belgian Congo	16.60 Fr.	0.38	1949
Doula, French Cameroons	45 CFA Fr.	0.39	1948
French Togoland	30-53 CFA Fr.	0.26-0.48	1948
Dakar, French West Africa	108 CFA Fr.	0.94	1948
Sudan, French West Africa	64 CFA Fr.	0.56	1948
Niger, French West Africa	42 CFA Fr.	0.37	1948
Gambia	2 S. 3d.	0.45	1948
Gold Coast	1S. 6d. - 3S. 3d.	0.30-0.65	1948
Gold Coast	2S. 9d. - 3S. 3d.	0.55-0.65	1949
Nigeria	9d. - 2S. 11d.	0.15-0.60	1948
Nigeria	9d. - 3S. 6d.	0.15-0.70	1949
Sierra Leone	1S. 8d. - 25.2d.	0.33-1.43	1949

Source: United Nations, Department of Economic Affairs,
Review of Economic Conditions in Africa, (New York: March
1951).

Wage Rates of Skilled Workers--Selected West African Countries, 1948 or 1949

Country	Daily Wage (local currency)	Daily Wage (U.S. dollars)	Industry or Occupation	Year
Gold Coast	0/3/5-0/5/0	0.65-1.00	Miners Min. 0/2/6-0/7/9	1948 and 1949
Nigeria	0/3/4-0/4/6	0.66-0.90	Gov't Clerical workers	1948
	0/4/6-0/9/6	0.90-1.90	Min. 6/0/0 per mo. Mining Min. 4/4/6 per month	1949
Sierra Leone	0/3/4-0/11/2	0.66-2.23		1949
French West Africa	2,735-7250(a)	23.52-62.61(a)	Artisans	1948

(a) Monthly Wage

Source: United Nations, Department of Economic Affairs, Review of Economic Conditions in Africa (New York: March, 1951).

Representative Hours and Wages in Selected Liberian
Industries and Occupations, January, 1953

Employer and Occupation	Hours per Week	Wage (Dollars) Entrance	Maximum	Time Unit
Government:				
Artisans:				
Highly Skilled	48	75.00	up	Month
Semi-skilled	48	20.00	32.00	"
Transport:				
Mechanics	48	42.00	60.00	"
Drivers	48	32.00	50.00	"
Laborers:	48	12.00	15.00	"
Clerical:				
Steno-typist	48	75.00	125.00	"
Typist	48	60.00	100.00	"
Rubber Plantations:				
Artisans:				
Highly Skilled	48	.50	2.60	Day
Semi-skilled	48	.25	.50	"
Transport:				
Mechanics	48	.50	1.69	"
Drivers	48	.50	2.16	"
Laborers:	48	.25	--	"

Representative Hours and Wages in Selected Liberian Industries and Occupations Continued

Employer and Occupation	Hours per Week	Wage (Dollars)		Time Unit
		Entrance	Maximum	
Clerical:				
Steno-typist	48	2.00	3.50	Day
Typist	48	1.00	2.00	"
Mining:				
Artisans:				
Highly Skilled	60	.16	.32	Hour
Semi-skilled	60	.08	.08	"
Transport:				
Mechanic s	60	.16	.32	"
Drivers	60	.08	.28	"
Laborers:	60	.04	.05	"
Clerical:				
Steno-typist	60	.25	.48	"
Typist	60	.25	.25	"
Construction:				
Artisans:				
Highly Skilled	48	.25	.37	"
Semi-skilled	48	.15	.20	"

Representative Hours and Wages in Selected Liberian
Industries and Occupations   Continued

Employer and Occupation	Hours per Week	Wage (Dollars)		Time Unit
		Entrance	Maximum	
Transport:				
Mechanics	48	.10	.50	Hour
Drivers	48	.15	.25	"
Laborers:	48	.05	.10	"
Clerical:				
Typist	48	.38	.38	"
Skilled Clerk	48	.35	.45	"

Source: American Embassy, Legation Dispatch No. 270,
(Monrovia: March 25, 1953).

Technical Assistance to Liberia, 1963--Positions
Offered and Supplied by Sector, Part A

Sector	Positions Offered	Positions Supplied
Agriculture	37	33
Forestry	17	17
Education	311	293
Public Health	15	13
Transportation & Communication	5	4
Government Organization, Public Safety	113	110
TOTAL	498	470

Technical Assistance to Liberia, 1963--Positions
Offered and Supplied by Donor, Part B

Donor	Positions Offered	Positions Supplied
USAID	114	96
Peace Corps	283	283
FAO	17	13
UNESCO	6	6
WHO	14	12
ILO	2	0
ICAO	3	2
UNTA	3	3
UN	3	3
China	19	19
Germany	24	24
UK	5	4
France	5	5
TOTAL	498	470

Source: Office of National Planning, Annual Report, 1962-1963,
(Monrovia: 1963).

SELECTED BIBLIOGRAPHY

BIBLIOGRAPHY

This bibliography contains only works which refer specifically to Liberia and which are basic sources of data relating to the Liberian economy. Excluded are the countless number of books and articles which treat economic development, foreign investment, and foreign aid either in general or with particular reference to countries other than Liberia. Also excluded are manufacturing works about Liberia, which unfortunately had to be omitted because of limitations of space.

BOOKS AND PERIODICALS

American Assembly, The United States and Africa, (New York: The American Assembly, 1958).

Anderson, R. Earle, Liberia, America's African Friend, (Chapel Hill: University of North Carolina Press, 1952).

Bennett, Jack, Small Business in Liberia, (Washington: The Continental-Allied Company, 1956).

Brown, George W., The Economic History of Liberia, (Washington: The Associated Publishers, Inc., 1947).

Buell, Raymond, Liberia: A Century of Survival, 1947-1947, (Philadelphia: University of Pennsylvania Press, 1947).

Burke, Fred G., Africa's Quest for Order, (Englewood Cliffs, New Jersey: Prentice-Hall, Inc., 1964).

Church, R. J. Harrison, West Africa, 2nd ed., (London: Longmans, Green and Co., Ltd., 1960).

Cole, Henry B., The Liberian Year Book, 1956, (London: The Diplomatic Press and Publishing Co., 1956).

Cole, Henry B., The Liberian Year Book, 1962 (London: The Diplomatic Press and Publishing Co., 1962).

Firestone, Harvey S., America Should Grow Its Own Rubber, (Akron: May 15, 1923).

Firestone, H. S., Jr. "Private Enterprise and Point Four-Firestone Tire and Rubber Company Plantations,"

Vital Speeches, 19, November 15, 1952, pp. 92-94.

Firestone, Harvey S. and Crowther, Samuel, Man and Rubber, (Garden City: Doubleday, Page and Company, 1926).

Firestone Plantations Company, Liberia and Firestone, (Akron: 1955).

Frankel, S. Herbert, The Economic Impact on Under-Developed Societies, (Cambridge, Mass: Harvard University Press, 1953).

Hanson, Earl P., "An Economic Survey of the Western Province of Liberia," Geographical Review, 37, January 1947, pp. 53-69.

Hanson, Earl P., "Missionaries and the Foreign Economic Administration," Address delivered in Monrovia, July 19, 1945.

Hanson, Earl P., "Problems of Liberia's Economic Development," Address delivered in Monrovia, January 14, 1945.

Harley, George W., "Masks as Agents of Social Control in Northeast Liberia," Peabody Papers, (XXXII), 1950.

Harley, George W., Native African Medicine, (Cambridge, Mass: Harvard University Press, 1941).

Harley, G. W. and Schwab, George, Tribes of the Liberian Hinterland, (Cambridge, Mass: The Museum, 1947).

Herskovits, Melville J., Economic Anthropology, (New York: Alfred A. Knopf, 1952).

Herskovits, M. J. and Harwitz, Mitchell, Economic Transition in Africa, (Evanston: Northwestern University Press, 1964).

Herskovits, M. J., The Human Factor in Changing Africa, (New York: Alfred A. Knopf, 1962).

Huberich, Charles E., The Political and Legislative History of Liberia, (New York: Central Book Company, 1947).

Kimble, George H. T. , Tropical Africa, (New York: The
Twentieth Century Fund, 1960), I & II.

Kindleberger, Charles P. , "The Terms of Trade and Economic
Development, " The Review of Economics and Statistics, XL,
Supplement, February, 1958, pp. 72-85.

League of Nations, Committee of the Council Appointed to
examine the Problem Raised by the Liberian Government's
Request for Assistance, Report of the Committee to the
Council, June 27, 1933, (League of Nations Doc. C. 421. M.
214. 1933. VII).

League of Nations, Committee of the Council Appointed to
examine the Problem Raised by the Liberian Government's
Request for Assistance, Report of the Committee to the
Council, May 21, 1932, (League of Nations Doc. C. 469. M. 238,
1932. VII).

League of Nations, Committee of the Council Appointed to
examine the Problem Raised by the Liberian Government's
Request for Assistance, Request for Assistance Submitted by
the Liberian Government, (League of Nations Doc. C. 662. M.
319. 1932. VII).

Lief, Alfred, The Firestone Story, (New York: Whittlesey
House, 1951).

Mead, Margaret, ed. , Cultural Patterns and Technical Change,
(New York: United Nations Economic and Social Council, 1955).

"Mission to Liberia, " Scientific American, 179, December, 1948,
p. 27.

Singer, W. W. , "The Distribution of Gains Between Investing
and Borrowing Countries, American Economic Review, XL,
May 1950, pp. 473-485.

Taylor, Wayne C. , The Firestone Operations In Liberia,
(Washington: National Planning Association, 1956).

Twe, Dihdwo, "Liberia, An American Responsibility, " Annals

of the American Academy of Political and Social Sciences, 282
July, 1952, pp. 104-107.

United Nations, Department of Economic and Social Affairs,
Economic Survey of Africa Since 1950, (New York: 1959).

United Nations, Department of Economic and Social Affairs,
Summary of Recent Developments in Africa, (New York: 1952).

LIBERIAN GOVERNMENT PUBLICATIONS

Joint United States-Liberia Commission for Economic
Development, A Proposed Nine-Year Program for the Economic
Development of Liberia, (Monrovia: 1955).

Republic of Liberia, Bureau of Statistics, Balance of Payments,
(Monrovia: Government Printing Office), Annual publications.

Republic of Liberia, Census of Population in Monrovia, CP
Report No. 0-1956, (Monrovia: Government Printing Office,
November 24, 1956).

Republic of Liberia, Census of Population in Monrovia, CP
Report No. 3-1956, (Monrovia: Government Printing Office,
December 31, 1956).

Republic of Liberia, Foreign Trade Supplement (Monrovia:
Government Printing Office), Annual publication.

Republic of Liberia, Department of Education, Survey of
Education, (Monrovia: 1963).

Republic of Liberia, Department of Interior, Bureau of Folkways, Traditional History, Customary Laws, Folkways and
Legends of the Vai Tribe, (Monrovia: 1963).

Republic of Liberia, Department of State, Acts Passed by the
Legislature of the Republic of Liberia (Monrovia: Government
Printing Office), Annual publication.

Republic of Liberia, Office of National Planning, Annual

Report (Monrovia), Annual publication.

Tubman, William V. S., Annual Message (Monrovia: 1964).

UNITED STATES GOVERNMENT PUBLICATIONS

Agency for International Development, AID Projects Active in
FY 1963, (Washington: Agency for International Development,
1964).

Agency for International Development, Operations Report:
Data as of December 31, 1964 , (Washington: Agency for International Development, 1965).

Department of Commerce, Bureau of Foreign Commerce,
Basic Data on the Liberian Economy, (Washington: GPO, 1955).

Department of Commerce,   Establishing a Business in Liberia,
(Washington, GPO, 1954).

Department of Commerce, Bureau of Foreign and Domestic
Commerce, Foreign Aid by the United States Government,
1940-1951, (Washington, GPO, 1952).

Department of Commerce, Office of International Trade,
Factors Limiting United States Investment Abroad, (Washington:
GPO, 1953).

Department of Commerce, United States Operations Mission
Dispatch No. A-112, (Monrovia: January 8, 1954).

Hanson, Earl P., Comments on the Five-Year Plan for the
Overall Development of the Republic of Liberia, 1946-1950,
(Monrovia: April 8, 1946).

Holsoe, Torkel, Forestry Progress and Timbering Opportunities
in the Republic of Liberia, (Washington: Government Printing
Office, 1955).

Litsey, Weldon, Annual Economic Review of Liberia, 1952,
(American Embassy, Monrovia: Legation Dispatch No. 64,

September 22, 1953).

Mayer, Karl R. , _Forest Resources of Liberia_, Department of Agriculture, (Washington: GPO, October,1951).

Meier, Oscar, _Liberia Annual Economic Report and Summary of Current Economic Information_, (American Legation, Monrovia: Legation Dispatch No. 156, September 23, 1948).

Orton, Clayton R. , _Agriculture of Liberia_, (Washington: GPO, February 14, 1954).

Department of State, _Labor Conditions in Liberia_, (Foreign Service Report, Monrovia: March 16, 1950).

Department of State, _Statement of Understanding Between the Government of Liberia and the Government of the United States_, (Washington: December 20, 1950).

Department of State, _Office of Intelligence Research, Post-War Economic Aid to Africa by the US, IBRD, and UN_, (Washington: December 29, 1952).

Export-Import Bank of Washington, _Semi-annual Report to Congress, January-June, 1949_, (Washington: Government Printing Office, 1949).

Foreign Economic Administration, Liberia Field Staff, _A Proposed Five-Year Program for the Economic Development of Liberia, and Memorandum Made Thereon by the Government of the Republic of Liberia_, (Monrovia: 1950).

Foreign Economic Administration, _Report on the Dimeh-Amino Project_, (Monrovia: March 26, 1946).

Foreign Economic Administration, _Summary Programs Report of Technical Assistance Activities_, Nov. 22, 1944 - May 1, 1946, (Monrovia: May 24, 1946).

Foreign Operations Administration, _Liberian Swamp Rice Production a Success_, (Washington: Government Printing Office, April, 1955).

Foreign Operations Administration, Resource Data Compiled by the Operation Mission in Liberia for the FAO Evaluation Team, (Monrovia: October 26, 1953).

Sly, John F. and Heddon, Walter P., The Free Port and Harbor of Monrovia, Republic of Liberia, (Washington: March 1, 1954).

Steadman, Robert F. , Report on the Fiscal System of Liberia, (Monrovia: July 11, 1952).